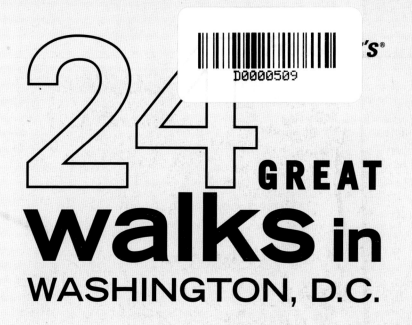

24 GREAT walks in WASHINGTON, D.C.

WILEY

Wiley Publishing, Inc.

Author: Carolyn Crouch
Series Editor: Donna Wood
Art Editor: Alison Fenton
Copy Editors: Polly Boyd and Helen Ridge
Proofreader: Fiona Wild
Picture Research: Luped Picture Research
Cartography provided by the Mapping Services
Department of AA Publishing
Image retouching and internal repro: Michael Moody
Production: Stephanie Allen

Edited, designed and produced by AA Publishing.
© Automobile Association Developments Limited 2009

All rights reserved. No part of this publication may be
reproduced, stored in a retrieval system, or transmitted
in any form or by any means – electronic, photocopying,
recording or otherwise – unless the written permission
of the publishers has been obtained beforehand. This
book may not be lent, resold, hired out or otherwise
disposed of by way of trade in any form of binding
other than that in which it is published, without the prior
consent of the publisher.

Published by AA Publishing.

Published in the United States by
Wiley Publishing, Inc.
111 River Street, Hoboken, NJ 07030

Find us online at Frommers.com

Frommer's is a registered trademark of Arthur Frommer.
Used under license.

Mapping © MAIRDUMONT/Falk Verlag 2008
ISBN 978-0-4704-5371-1

A03625

A CIP catalogue record for this book is available from the
British Library.

The contents of this publication are believed correct
at the time of printing. Nevertheless, the publishers
cannot accept responsibility for errors or omissions,
or for changes in details given in this guide or for
the consequences of any reliance on the information
provided by the same. Assessments of attractions and
so forth are based upon the author's own experience
and, therefore, descriptions given in this guide necessarily
contain an element of subjective opinion which may not
reflect the publishers' opinion or dictate a reader's own
experiences on another occasion.

Colour reproduction by Keene Group, Andover
Printed in China by Leo Paper Group

San Mateo
Public Library

OPPOSITE: THOMAS JEFFERSON MEMORIAL

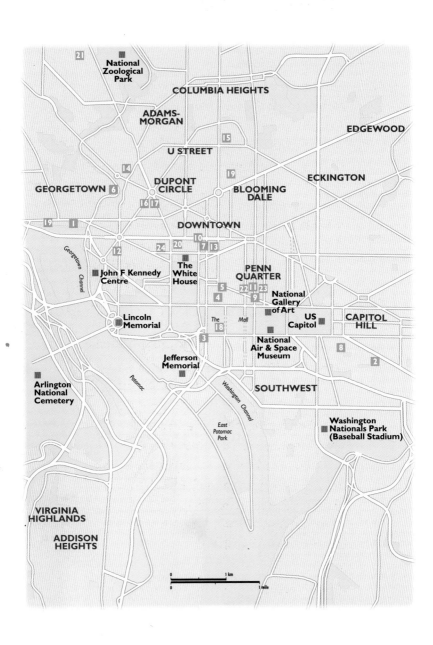

21

National
Zoological
Park

COLUMBIA HEIGHTS

ADAMS-
MORGAN

EDGEWOOD

15

U STREET

19

ECKINGTON

14

GEORGETOWN 6

DUPONT
CIRCLE

BLOOMING
DALE

16 17

DOWNTOWN

19 1

10

12

24 20

7 13

John F Kennedy
Centre

The
White
House

PENN
QUARTER

5

22 11 23

4

9

National
Gallery
of Art

Lincoln
Memorial

The   Mall

US
Capitol

CAPITOL
HILL

18

8

3

National
Air & Space
Museum

2

Jefferson
Memorial

Arlington
National
Cemetery

SOUTHWEST

Georgetown Channel

Potomac

Washington Channel

East
Potomac
Park

Washington
Nationals Park
(Baseball Stadium)

VIRGINIA
HIGHLANDS

ADDISON
HEIGHTS

0   1 km
0   1 mile

CONTENTS

Introduction 6

1 On the Georgetown Waterfront 8
2 At Home on Capitol Hill 14
3 Tidal Basin Memorials and Cherry Trees 22
4 A Visit to the Memorial Sites 30
5 A Walk along America's Grand Avenue 38
6 Great Estates of Georgetown 44
7 Scandals in the Presidents' Backyard 50
8 A Walk through the Corridors of Power 56
9 Washington during the Civil War 66
10 The Tragic Death of a Revered President 73
11 Urban Scavenger Hunt in Penn Quarter 78
12 History and Culture in Foggy Bottom 84
13 Elegant Circles and Squares 92
14 A Feast for the Senses at Kalorama 100
15 Duke Ellington's Washington 106
16 Gracious Homes and Vibrant Streets 112
17 Grandes Dames of Embassy Row 120
18 The Best-kept Smithsonian Secrets 128
19 The Kennedys in Georgetown 136
20 The Haunted Houses of Lafayette Square 140
21 An Oasis of Peace and Calm 148
22 Blazing the Sculpture Trail 154
23 Washington's Niche Museums 160
24 International Washington 166

Index 174
Acknowledgements 176

Introduction

Washington, DC, known as 'DC', is renowned for its memorials, museums and politics. Even those who have never visited the US can probably identify the Capitol building, the White House and the soaring obelisk known as the Washington Monument. For US citizens and international visitors alike, the lure of a trip to Washington is the chance to take the pulse of America's political process, seeing for themselves where and how the wheels of one of the world's largest democracies turn, as well as making the pilgrimage to commemorate figures from the past who dedicated their lives to advancing principles of freedom, justice and equality.

Yet consider another popular American saying: 'There's no place like home'. Washington is hometown to half a million people who revel in an urban life, complete with pedestrian-friendly streets, an extensive subway system, 19th-century townhouses, and shops, bars and restaurants galore. This is the Washington that can capture the imagination and win the heart of any visitor who is willing to take the time to explore beyond the sweeping National Mall. You'll be amazed by the estates and large gardens that remain intact as Washington has grown up around them, and when it comes to the buildings, hints of the past nestle intriguingly among sparkling new developments – two centuries of Washington life, past and present, co-existing happily side by side.

This is the Washington you'll discover in the walking tours found in this guide. Fear not – the majestic memorials and other famous sites are included, as are the lesser-known byways and buildings that surprise even Washington residents. Many of the walks in this book place you smack in the middle of the US capital at work, while others introduce you to the breathtaking areas beyond the city centre. Casual strolls among the city's hidden gems such as out-of-the-way museums, outdoor sculptures or alleyways lined with tiny houses complement grander walks along majestic Pennsylvania Avenue or through elegant Lafayette Square.

If you have only a day or two in Washington, make sure to choose a walk that includes sites along the National Mall. Then select one of the

thematic excursions that convey an aspect of the city that is unfamiliar to you. It's vital to take a stroll through at least one residential area, because it is in these neighbourhoods that you'll find some of the best reasons to return to Washington again and again.

Eat whenever and wherever you can. Washington residents will tell you that the city's culinary scene offers an abundance of appealing options, from ethnic food served in humble surroundings to cosy cafés, hip bars and award-winning restaurants. In warm weather, stop by one of the numerous weekly farmers' markets. Nearly all the eateries recommended in this guide are owned and operated by Washingtonians, allowing you to experience local colour and local flavour simultaneously.

Keep your eyes open as you soak up Washington on foot. Although relatively young compared with other world capitals, Washington celebrates its two centuries of history almost everywhere you look – on plaques, heritage markers, statues or during the vibrant festivals that seem to occur almost every weekend. This guide can tell only some of the stories, so delight in the serendipity of discovering others as you walk. You'll quickly realize that all it requires is a step or two, and you're on the way to making Washington your own.

WHERE TO EAT

$	=	Inexpensive
$$	=	Moderate
$$$	=	Expensive

On the Georgetown Waterfront

Quaint houses, river walks and tiny alleyways tell the story of a once-thriving waterfront community on the banks of the Potomac River.

Named after King George II of England, 'George' was the original name of the small Maryland town founded in 1751. Thanks to its location, Georgetown became a bustling port and, throughout the 18th century, it was a busy, gritty place, with wharves and rowdy taverns. However, by the 1820s the Potomac River had become filled with silt, and the advent of steam navigation meant that cities with deeper natural ports captured much of the river trade. By the early 20th century, the Georgetown economy had reinvented itself in the form of mills built along the waterfront. On this walk, you'll see the façades of some of these buildings, formerly operating as a power plant, flour and paper mills and an incinerator. They are interspersed with terraced houses that continue to be family homes and small businesses. Today's Georgetown waterfront is a fascinating amalgamation of hidden alleyways, narrow streets, and commercial office buildings. It is also the site of the longest National Park in the US.

Exiting the Foggy Bottom Metro, turn left and proceed to Washington Circle. Turn left and walk around the circle, exiting onto Pennsylvania Avenue, NW by bearing left. Follow Pennsylvania Avenue to the intersection of 28th Street, NW. Follow M Street, NW for two blocks, crossing 28th and 29th Streets, NW. At 30th Street, NW turn left. About mid-block on your left, find a white house at No. 1068.

This house is typical of the Federal-style brick houses that were built throughout Georgetown between 1790 and 1820, although the residences found along the waterfront are usually substantially smaller than their cousins north of M Street. Like many in this area, this house was raised when the Chesapeake & Ohio (C & O) Canal was built in 1850; the original ground floor is now below street level. Look out for star emblems on the sides of buildings. Until the mid-19th century, structures were held together with a cast-iron pole running from wall to wall, and the ends were secured on the exterior using a cast-iron tie rod, usually in the form of a decorative star. This helped maintain the integrity of structures that were more than one storey tall.

Walk downhill on 30th Street until you come to the C & O Canal lock No. 3 on your right. Turn right onto the towpath.

A ceremony to celebrate the start of construction of the C & O Canal took place in Georgetown on 4 July 1828, amid much fanfare. It began as a speculative development to link the eastern seaports with the Ohio River and the plan was to extend all the way inland to Pittsburgh, Pennsylvania. However, funding for the project did not follow and the canal never got as far as the Ohio River.

When work ceased in 1852, the C & O Canal stretched 185 miles (300km) from Georgetown to Cumberland, Maryland (about half the distance originally planned). In its heyday, for over half a decade, the canal was a lifeline for communities and businesses along the Potomac River. Coal, lumber, grain and other agricultural products floated down the canal to market. However, by 1924 the canal was obsolete – floods had devastated the waterway, and it was no longer considered of economic use because railways provided cheaper transportation. The canal was abandoned until 1971, when it came under the jurisdiction of the National Historic Park Service and was subsequently restored. During the summer months, the canal relives its past and the public can enjoy mule-drawn barge rides. The C & O Canal Visitors Center also offers guided tours of Georgetown and lectures. The bust on the pedestal along the canal is of US Supreme Court Justice William O. Douglas, who successfully crusaded to save the Georgetown portion of the canal in the 1940s.

C & O NATIONAL HISTORIC PARK;
www.nps.gov/choh

OPPOSITE: BARGE RIDES ON THE C & O CANAL ARE AVAILABLE TO THE PUBLIC

DISTANCE **3 miles (4.8km)**

ALLOW **2.5 hours**

START **Foggy Bottom Metro station**

FINISH **Foggy Bottom Metro station**

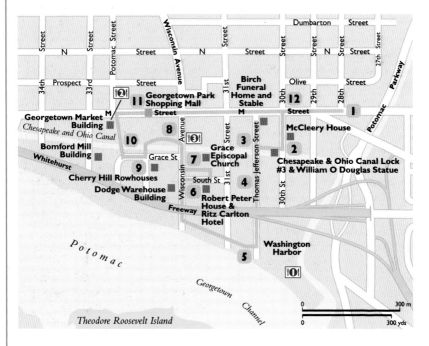

3 Follow the towpath to the intersection of Thomas Jefferson Street, NW. Turn right and proceed to No. 1069 on your right.

This house is another classic example of Federal-style architecture. Notice how the house has two doorways, one leading to a former shop on the ground floor and the other to the residence on the upper two floors. The shop door, originally to the left of the existing door, was bricked up during renovations

in 1941. Just up the way is the former Birch Funeral Home and Stable at 1083 Thomas Jefferson Street. The building with the garage was the stable for the funeral home, which was located just around the corner at M Street. The stable is considered to be the only late 19th-century structure of its kind left in the Georgetown waterfront area. By 1891, Joseph Birch had died, leaving the business to his sons, George and Isaac. It remained in the family until the property was sold in 1966.

4 Head away from M Street down Thomas Jefferson Street. You will pass over the C & O Canal and then under the elevated Whitehurst Freeway. Cross busy K Street, NW and proceed into Washington Harbor until you reach the Potomac River.

'Xanadu on the Potomac' was how one Washington arbiter of taste described Washington Harbor – a huge complex of shops, offices and condominiums created by US architect Arthur Cotton Moore (born 1935) in 1986. The merits of the development aside, it's the sweeping views that grab your attention. Looking from left to right you can pick out Thompson's Boat Center (which rents out kayaks and canoes), the curved façade of the Watergate Complex (a famous residential building), the gleaming white John F. Kennedy Center for the Performing Arts, Theodore Roosevelt Island directly across the way, and to the right the Francis Scott Key Memorial Bridge connecting Georgetown to Virginia.

5 Follow the path through the park. At K Street, NW (beneath the Whitehurst Freeway), cross the street and begin to walk up the hill of Wisconsin Avenue, NW. Stop to look at 1000 Wisconsin Avenue, immediately on your left.

Originally a warehouse, this building was constructed in 1800 by two merchant brothers, Ebenezer and Francis Dodge, whose family epitomized the successful merchant class of early Georgetown. With

WHERE TO EAT

🍽 **AGRARIA,**
3000 K Street, NW;
Tel: 1-202-298-0003.
This Washington Harbor restaurant provides not only a view to the Potomac River but also dishes made with ingredients procured from family farms across the US. **$$$**

🍽 **DEAN & DELUCA,**
3276 M Street, NW;
Tel: 1-202-342-2500.
From produce to pastries to prepared meals to take away, this high-end food emporium also offers light fare at its outdoor patio. **$$**

🍽 **FILOMENA,**
1063 Wisconsin Avenue, NW;
Tel: 1-202-337-2782.
A Georgetown institution for over 20 years, offering traditional Italian food near the C & O Canal. **$$**

their own fleet of schooners, the Dodge brothers brought sugar and molasses into Georgetown, trading tobacco, flour and lime. After the death of Francis in 1851, the brothers' two sons continued the tradition of trade with the West Indies, but by 1857 they were bankrupt.

6 Walk a bit further up Wisconsin Avenue and then turn right onto South Street, NW. Follow it until you see the Ritz Carlton Hotel complex on the right at 3134–3136 South Street.

A small wooden chapel was constructed on this site in 1855, but it was later razed and replaced with the stone church that you see today. It was founded to serve the labourers, craftsmen, shopkeepers and boatmen who lived in this tiny district known as Brickyard Hill because it was built on the site of the old brickworks. An 1895 edition of the *Washington Evening Star* reported, 'It is the only church here in a really poor district and whenever its pastor is not in the pulpit or fulfilling his own immediate wants he is out among his people dispensing aid to the unfortunate.' Outreach continues to be integral to the parish identity: the Georgetown Ministry Center for the Homeless is based here, as well as a Montessori nursery.

8 Exit the churchyard and cross Wisconsin Avenue. Notice the commemorative plaque for the C & O Canal outside the entrance to the Georgetown Park shopping mall. Cross the pedestrian bridge to the left of the mall entrance over onto Grace Street, NW. Follow it to the intersection of the Cecil Place alley. Walk into the alley to view the terraced houses at 1033–1043 Cecil Place.

The house facing the street was the home of the first mayor of Georgetown, Robert Peter. Originally from Scotland, Peter arrived in what was then called 'George Town' and quickly became a wealthy tobacco merchant and landholder; he became mayor in 1790. This house and the building behind it were both moved in July 1999 so as not to be in the way of construction for the Ritz Carlton Hotel. After the restoration work, the historic buildings were returned to the site and now house the hotel's administrative offices. The hotel itself is built around what was once the DC incinerator plant – the smokestack is still in evidence.

These houses were part of Cherry Hill, a residential area that would have been entirely separate from Brickyard Hill across Wisconsin Avenue. Speculators built simple structures like these in the middle of the 19th century to accommodate a growing population of workers seeking low-cost housing. Such was the demand that this area was filled

7 Turn and cross South Street, climbing the small staircase to Grace Episcopal Church at 1041 Wisconsin Avenue.

in with terraces between 1870 and 1890. Each house is exactly 24ft (7.3m) long and 12ft (3.6m) wide, with a garden at the back. Today, given their Georgetown address, the houses are no longer inexpensive or lived in by labourers, but they are a poignant reminder of a bygone era of Washington's working waterfront.

9 Follow Grace Street until you reach an area that opens out to the C & O Canal. On your left is a large white building known as the Bomford Mill.

Colonel George Bomford operated a flour mill here from 1832 until 1844, when it was destroyed by fire. He then erected a cotton mill on the ruins. A number of mills were sited along the Georgetown waterfront in order to take advantage of the steep drop to the river. Notice the rod stars on the façade.

10 Turn around and cross the pedestrian bridge over the C & O Canal. Climb the stairs and walk along the plaza between the Georgetown Park shops and Dean & DeLuca market. The front entrance to the market is at 3276 M Street, NW.

Butcher's Market, the earliest Georgetown public market, was established before the American War of Independence (1775–83). Since then, this site has always accommodated a market of some sort. The current building, which dates from the early 1800s, also served as the site for meetings of Georgetown's early commissioners. In 1992 it became Dean & DeLuca, the gourmet grocer from New York City. In warm weather, there's nothing more enjoyable than sitting out on the adjoining patio and sampling the offerings while (on Sunday mornings) listening to live jazz.

11 The route back to the walk start point takes you along M Street, Georgetown's busy commercial thoroughfare. Nearly every building you pass is historic, but the one to stop at is 3051 M Street. The Old Stone House is a National Park site.

The Old Stone House was built in 1765, making it the oldest structure built in Washington. Christopher Layman, a cabinetmaker, used the charming granite building as both a residence and a shop. After his death, the house was sold to Cassandra Chew, who added the rear wing in 1767. Until it was purchased by the federal government in 1953, the building had been continuously used as a residence or a residence and shop. It is one of the few examples in Washington of American vernacular architecture that predates the American War of Independence.

12 To return to Foggy Bottom Metro, turn left into M Street as you exit the building grounds. Follow M Street to 28th Street, where it changes its name to Pennsylvania Avenue. Follow Pennsylvania Avenue to Washington Circle, bearing right to walk around the circle. Exit the circle by turning right into 23rd Street. The station is on the right, halfway down the block.

At Home on Capitol Hill

Nestled next to the US Capitol is Capitol Hill, where long-time residents and newcomers alike relish their unique place in the city's urban identity.

Although the outside world may associate Capitol Hill solely with the US Congress, those who make Washington their home conjure up a very different image: that of a vibrant area spread across one of the largest historic districts in the country and filled with quaint terraces, leafy parks, shops, cafes, churches and schools. Pride in the place is evident in the careful restoration and loving upkeep bestowed upon the 19th-century homes, adorned with flowerbeds and shrubs. Although many of the stately townhouses seen on this walk were not built until after the US Civil War (1861–65), Capitol Hill is nonetheless one of Washington's oldest areas, its first development occurring during the late 1790s, just as the federal government prepared to locate here permanently. It proved an attractive area for those who desired to live near to where they worked. Over the years, though, the allure of life on 'the Hill' has been such that Washingtonians with no connection to congressional matters have been eager to call it home.

From Eastern Market Metro station, cross 7th Street, SE at the public library and proceed along D Street, SE. Look for No. 619 on the right.

A social-service organization called Friendship House occupies this site today, but you can see the roof of the original house through the entry court. The Maples was an estate constructed between 1795 and 1806 for a wealthy trader named William Mayne Duncanson, who would have appreciated the peace and quiet provided by what was, at the time, a tranquil woodland environment. Capitol Hill was undergoing a development spurt when pioneering journalist Emily Edson Briggs (the first woman to receive White House press credentials) purchased The Maples in 1870. She added 21 rooms to the house and decorated it with artefacts and treasures obtained on her many travels abroad. In 1936, her heirs sold the house to an anonymous buyer, who in turn donated it to Friendship House.

2 Continue along D Street to 6th Street, SE. Turn right. Take note of Mr Henry's, a venerable Capitol Hill pub known for its live jazz, at the intersection of 6th Street and Pennsylvania Avenue, SE. Turn left. Follow Pennsylvania Avenue past Seward Square on the right. At the corner of Pennsylvania Avenue and 4th Street, SE look for 330 Pennsylvania Avenue.

The Naval Lodge Building was constructed in 1895 as a meeting place

WHERE TO EAT

|O| MARKET LUNCH,
Eastern Market,
7th Street, SE;
Tel: 1-202-547-8444.
Crab cakes, eggs and grits, and blueberry buckwheat pancakes are just a few of the favourites served at this popular lunch counter. $

|O| MONTMARTRE,
327 7th Street, SE;
Tel: 1-202-544-1244.
A cheerful French bistro near Eastern Market. $$

|O| SONOMA,
223 Pennsylvania Avenue, SE;
Tel: 1-202-544-8088.
The Sonoma Valley in Northern California is the inspiration for this romantic wine bar. $$

for Naval Lodge No. 4. The organization, which continues to meet twice-monthly in a stately space upstairs, is proud to reside in the oldest Masonic structure in the city. The Lodge makes its space available throughout the year for the popular Ruth Ann Overbeck Lecture Series, named after a beloved Hill resident and historian. Focusing on the history of Capitol Hill, the lectures draw residents from throughout the city.

3 From the Lodge, turn left onto 4th Street, SE and continue to Independence Avenue, SE. Turn right,

OPPOSITE: BEAUTIFULLY MAINTAINED BRICK TERRACE HOUSES, TYPICAL OF CAPITOL HILL

DISTANCE 1 mile (1.6km)

ALLOW 1.5 hours (more with site visits)

START Eastern Market Metro station

FINISH Eastern Market Metro station

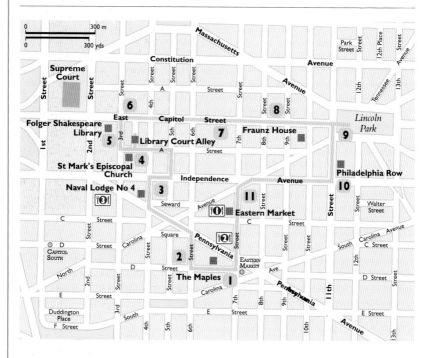

then one block later turn left onto 5th Street, SE. Next, turn left onto A Street, SE. Between 4th and 3rd Streets, look for the entrance to Library Court alley.

By the end of the 19th century, over 300 residential alleys such as Library Court existed. Many had been developed following the US Civil War, when the city swelled with new arrivals seeking low-cost housing. They often found it in these tiny two-up, two-down houses. By the 1920s, the alleys were notorious for their overcrowded, basic conditions: many lacked indoor plumbing and electricity. Large numbers were torn down and their sites redeveloped with more expensive houses. On Capitol Hill, however, alley houses can still be found and are considered a quiet, off-the-beaten-path alternative to the hurried pace of city life.

4 Double back to A Street. Across from the Library Court entrance is St Mark's Episcopal Church.

In the mid-1960s, as older couples moved out of Capitol Hill, middle-class families, attracted to the area's relatively cheap homes, Victorian architecture and community spirit, moved in with ideals and energy. St Mark's Church was a gathering place for this 'back to the city' movement of young, white families who became intensely involved with one another and their new-found community. The Romanesque Revival church building was constructed here in 1889. St Mark's continues to be an integral part of Capitol Hill life. The St Mark's Players are the church's resident theatre group, the St Mark's Dance Studio offers classes to the public, as does the St Mark's Yoga Center. The church Arts Council brings together visual artists, writers, architects and needleworkers.

5 From the church, turn right onto 3rd Street. At the intersection of 3rd and East Capitol Streets is the Folger Shakespeare Library on the left.

Henry Clay Folger (1857–1930), a millionaire Standard Oil executive, devoted a great deal of his life to the acquisition of what is now the largest collection of Shakespearean materials in the world. Perhaps the most famous work in his collection is the first edition of Shakespeare's works, printed in 1623 and known as the *First Folio*. Out of a world supply of 238 First Folios, Folger collected 79 copies, one of which is always on display in the Great Hall of the Shakespeare Library. A recreated Elizabethan theatre is still used for live performances. Notice the nine bas-relief panels depicting scenes from Shakespeare's plays on the library's main façade.

FOLGER SHAKESPEARE LIBRARY;
MON–SAT 10–5; www.folger.edu

6 Stop to admire East Capitol Street, then follow the avenue to No. 506, which will be on the left.

Following the US Civil War, members of the large, stable government workforce found Capitol Hill a convenient area to live in. The resulting building boom accounts for the majestic terraces found on East Capitol Street. This broad avenue, stretching from the Capitol to the Potomac River, was conceived to be 160ft (48m) wide. When it was finally constructed in 1870, a 50ft (15m) road was paved down the middle, leaving

55ft (17m) garden strips on either side. These represent one of the chief benefits of owning a home on East Capitol Street. The house at No. 506 was built in 1873, but by 1887 it had been completely remodelled, lending it the Romanesque Revival style that is still evident today. The prominent bay window is referred to as a pressed-tin oriel. The ability to press and form materials, including brick, gave late 19th-century homeowners a myriad of choices in the appearance of their homes and made possible the projecting towers and bays seen on many of these homes.

7 Continue on East Capitol Street four blocks to No. 923 on the right.

The Fraunz house, built in 1892, is a classic Queen Anne-style terraced townhouse. Unlike the exuberant 'painted ladies' of San Francisco, the Queen Anne-style houses on Capitol Hill reflected the conservative tastes of their middle-class occupants. The style, which was popular in the US between 1860 and 1910, is distinguished by bays and towers or turrets topped by elaborate caps or, as in the case of this house, a pediment. This style of house is usually clad in timber and shingle, but on Capitol Hill pressed brick was the preferred architectural material.

8 Follow East Capitol Street across 10th and 11th Streets, SE then cross into Lincoln Park.

This is one of the best spots to observe day-to-day life of Capitol Hill residents, whether they are out walking dogs, attending their children at the playground or staying in shape by jogging around the park's perimeter. Look for the Emancipation monument, unveiled in 1876 and depicting President Abraham Lincoln bidding a slave to rise to freedom. Opposite this sculpture is another that honours Mary McLeod Bethune, founder of the National Council of Negro Women (see Walk 13). It is the first memorial in Washington dedicated to an African-American leader as well as the first to honour an American woman.

9 Return to 11th Street from the park and turn left. Cross East Capitol Street by the dry cleaning shop on the corner. Continue to 124–154 11th Street.

These 16 terraced houses are associated with one of Capitol Hill's most enduring urban legends. The story goes that developer Charles Gessford built them to resemble townhouses in Philadelphia in order to soothe his wife's homesickness for her native city. While the Philadelphia connection is accurate, the name of the developer is not. In fact, Philadelphia tugboat manufacturer Stephen Flanagan constructed the houses in 1862 on speculation. Flanagan may have been overly optimistic in selecting this location, because it was 30 years before this part of Capitol Hill became populated with residents and it took until 1897 for Flanagan to sell the last of his houses.

10 Follow 11th Street to Independence Avenue, SE. Turn right and proceed to where 7th Street and North Carolina Avenue, SE intersect with Independence Avenue. Turn left onto 7th Street. You will be by Eastern Market.

Many consider Eastern Market to be the heart and soul of Capitol Hill. This is where the local residents gather to shake off the working week and fill up their larders – and stomachs! Completed in 1873, it was designed by Adolph Cluss, a prominent local architect. It is one of the few public markets left in the city, and the only one retaining its original public market function. Indoor vendors continue to sell flowers, produce, meat and bread seven days a week. At the weekend, they are joined outdoors by a lively farmers' and arts-and-crafts market. A severe fire destroyed the interior of Eastern Market on 30 April 2007. During its restoration, the vendors have been located in a temporary structure across the street from their original home, continuing to welcome the citizenry of Capitol Hill.

11 To get back to the Metro, follow 7th Street to Pennsylvania Avenue. Cross Pennsylvania Avenue and then turn left and cross 7th Street. Eastern Market station will be directly in front of you.

ABOVE: A CAPITOL HILL STOREFRONT WITH WARES DISPLAYED OUTSIDE AT WEEKENDS

STATUE OF MARY McLEOD BETHUNE AND AFRICAN-AMERICAN CHILDREN, LINCOLN PARK

Tidal Basin Memorials and Cherry Trees

A man-made creation of the late 19th century, the Tidal Basin is the site of several memorials. Surrounding it are thousands of flowering cherries.

If you embark on this walk in late March or early April, be prepared to share the path with happy hordes on their way to bask in the transient beauty of Washington's flowering Japanese cherry trees. Otherwise, this route can be appreciated for passing through a portion of the National Mall that does not attract constant crowds. It's best done in the early morning or late afternoon, when daylight allows you to read the various inscriptions and plaques. America's third president, Thomas Jefferson, is honoured here, and the life and times of President Franklin Delano Roosevelt is chronicled in a memorial that combines landscape architecture and sculptural forms. Virginian statesman George Mason sits peacefully amidst a garden setting, while the spirit of civil-rights champion Martin Luther King whispers through a site that is being prepared as a memorial to the country's greatest African-American leader. Discover the two original Japanese cherry trees, and glimpse the White House on Pennsylvania Avenue.

1 Upon exiting Smithsonian Metro station, turn left and proceed along Independence Avenue, SW past the Department of Agriculture buildings. Cross 14th Street, SW.

Many a visitor has mistaken this red-brick Romanesque-style building for the Smithsonian Castle, which is located a few blocks east. However, it actually houses the US Forest Service, as the Smokey the Bear figure often placed outside the 14th Street entrance would indicate. Originally constructed in 1880 for the Bureau of Printing and Engraving, it is now the oldest of the buildings comprising the Department of Agriculture (of which the Forest Service is part).

2 Continue along Independence Avenue, turning left at 15th Street, SW (Raoul Wallenberg Place). Walk about a quarter of a block on 15th Street.

Close to the National Mall, the US Holocaust Memorial Museum provides a powerful lesson about the 'fragility of freedom'. Architect James Ingo Freed (1930–2005), who was born in Germany but lived most of his life in the US, visited Holocaust sites, including camps and ghettos, as he was designing the building (completed in 1993). Above the entrance on Raoul Wallenberg Place – named after the Swedish diplomat who rescued thousands of Hungarian Jews – is a solitary window containing 16 solid 'panes' made of smooth, soft stone, each framed by clear glass, thus reversing the normal configuration and obscuring one's ability to look in or out. Joel Shapiro's sculpture *Loss and Regeneration* evokes the disintegration of families and of shattered lives. The larger piece is a towering, tree-like form. Nearby, a smaller, house-like structure is tipped upside-down on its roof. Shapiro created the piece to commemorate children who perished during the Holocaust.

US HOLOCAUST MEMORIAL MUSEUM;
DAILY 10–5.30; TEL: 1-202-488-0400;
www.ushmm.org

3 Proceed along 15th Street to the next building, the Bureau of Engraving and Printing.

You are standing outside the largest producer of security documents in the US. Although the building is best known for printing paper money, it also produces portions of US passports, military ID cards

23

DISTANCE 1.5 miles (2.5km)

ALLOW 2 hours (more with museum visit)

START Smithsonian Metro station (Independence Avenue exit)

FINISH Smithsonian Metro station (Independence Avenue entrance)

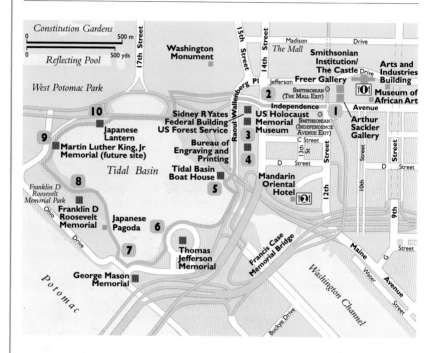

and Naturalization Certificates. Each document is designed and manufactured with 'counterfeit–deterrence' features. On a tour of the facility, you will learn that the average lifespan of a $1 bill is 21 months, and a $100 bill is 89 months. Schoolchildren seem to enjoy purchasing plastic containers of shredded dollars.

BUREAU OF ENGRAVING AND PRINTING;

TEL (FOR TOURS): 1-866-874-2330 (toll-free) or 1-202-874-2330 (local);

www.moneyfactory.gov

4 Continue to follow 15th Street to the end of the block. Carefully cross Maine Avenue, SW and walk over to the Tidal Basin boathouse.

After a severe flood damaged parts of the National Mall and Washington's waterfront in 1881, the Army Corps of Engineers were enlisted to manage the flow of the Potomac River. Accumulation of silt and debris made the river prone to flooding. The Potomac was dredged and the massive amounts of silt removed were used to create the peninsula known as East Potomac Park (to the left of where you are standing), this Tidal Basin, and the land west of the Washington Monument. The original purpose of the Tidal Basin was to flush water from the Potomac River through to the nearby Washington Channel. Today, the Tidal Basin provides the means for taking in the surrounding views by paddle boats, which can be rented during warm weather.

TIDAL BASIN PADDLE BOAT DOCK;

www.tidalbasinpaddleboats.com

5 Follow the path from the boathouse along the Tidal Basin until you reach the Thomas Jefferson memorial.

Very few significant Washington structures have come to life without a degree of controversy. In this case, the Thomas Jefferson Memorial Commission asked US architect John Russell Pope (1874–1937) to submit a design – without holding a nationwide competition. Many decried this approach, claiming that it went against all that democratically minded President Thomas Jefferson (1743–1826) held true. Pope proposed designing the memorial in the style of the Roman Pantheon, which Jefferson himself used for both his Virginia home, Monticello, and the school he founded, the University of Virginia. Washington's arbiters of taste and design, the Commission on Fine Arts, were dismayed by his proposal, though the Thomas Jefferson Commission was savvy enough to bypass their objections by appealing directly to President

WHERE TO EAT

🍽 CASTLE CAFÉ,
Smithsonian Castle Building,
1000 Jefferson Drive, SW;
Tel: 1-202-633-1000.
Enjoy casual offerings of sandwiches, salads and baked goods in one of the city's landmark structures. After your meal, wander around and soak up the Gothic Revival architecture. $

🍽 EMPRESS LOUNGE,
Mandarin Oriental Hotel,
1330 Maryland Avenue, SW;
Tel: 1-202-554-858.
For elegance and a view. The light-fare menu features Asian-inspired nibbles and signature martinis. A curry lunch buffet is available during the week. $$

Franklin D. Roosevelt. He gave his full support to the Commission and authorized the design, a somewhat controversial move for a US president. The memorial was finally unveiled on 13 April 1943, the bicentenary of Thomas Jefferson's birth. Along with a stately bronze likeness of the man himself (he holds a copy of the Declaration of Independence), the memorial contains four panels of famous quotations.

THOMAS JEFFERSON MEMORIAL;

www.nps.gov/thje

6 Follow the pathway as it runs up a small embankment. At the top, cross Ohio Drive, SW and walk into the garden across the street.

This perfectly poised figure is probably the least known of the Virginians who contributed so much to forge the founding principles of the US government when America gained independence from Britain in 1775. Despite having no formal education, statesman George Mason (1725–92) authored the Virginia Declaration of Rights, the document used as a model for many state constitutions, as well as France's Declaration of the Rights of Man and the United Nations Charter of the Rights of Man. Although he was directly involved in the composition of the US Constitution, he ultimately refused to sign it, because it did not abolish the slave trade and lacked an explicit statement of individual rights.

The sculptor and landscape designer of the memorial's garden reinterpreted an existing flower garden planted here in the 1920s with perennials, wooden benches, evergreens and boxwoods, each a tribute to the formal garden at Mason's home, Gunston Hall. What's particularly pleasing about the depiction of Mason is that a visitor can actually sit down next to Mason as a friend would. A very polite friend, that is, as Mason appears to be immersed in Cicero.

GEORGE MASON MEMORIAL;

www.nps.gov/gemm

7 After leaving the memorial garden, return to Ohio Drive, enjoying the view of the Tidal Basin and Potomac River atop the Inlet Bridge. You may be able to see the National Air Force memorial swooping upwards across the river in Virginia. Follow the pathway that takes you right along the Tidal Basin itself. Watch out for low-hanging Japanese cherry trees! Continue along this course until you reach a stairway leading up to the Franklin D. Roosevelt memorial. Walk around the building directly in front of you by first turning right and then left towards the entrance of the memorial itself.

It takes a memorial comprised of four 'rooms' to adequately chronicle the life and impact of America's only four-term president. Franklin D. Roosevelt (1882–1945) guided the country through two monumental events: the Great Depression and World War II. Inscriptions recall his speeches, often conveying what citizens themselves felt. Sculptures, such as the gaunt Depression-era couple and men standing in a bread line, depict a stark reality. Likenesses of Roosevelt himself and First Lady Eleanor Roosevelt embody the strength and resolve each brought to their respective role. Even Fala, Roosevelt's devoted Scottish Terrier, is on hand. Water flowing throughout the memorial evokes both Roosevelt's love of sailing and the healing pools he bathed in while attempting to rehabilitate his polio-stricken legs. When the memorial was unveiled in 1997, many wondered why the country's first disabled president had not been overtly depicted as such. In 2001, a new statue of Roosevelt in a wheelchair was placed at the entrance to the memorial.

FRANKLIN DELANO ROOSEVELT MEMORIAL; www.nps.gov/fdrm

27

8 Exit the Roosevelt memorial and then turn right, following the path along West Basin Drive, SW. Look out for a medium-sized bronze plaque placed in the ground on your righthand side.

This is the future site of the Martin Luther King memorial. Fundraising has been underway for a number of years and a design has been selected. Before his assassination in Memphis, Tennessee, Martin Luther King (1929–68) was the pivotal leader of the Civil Rights movement. A Baptist minister, King led the Montgomery, Alabama Bus Boycott and helped found the Southern Christian Leadership Conference. His eloquence and skill as a speechmaker soon established him as one of the greatest orators of the 20th century. In 1964, he became the youngest person to be awarded the Nobel Peace Prize. His death on 4 April 1968 plunged many US cities into days of violent riots, yet King's legacy of non-violent civil disobedience, his inspiring writings and his steadfast example have proven more enduring. His memorial will be the first on the National Mall dedicated to an African-American.

MARTIN LUTHER KING MEMORIAL SITE;
www.mlkmemorial.org

9 Follow the path to Independence Avenue, SW. Turn right and continue until you discover a large stone lantern on the right, just before the Kutz Bridge.

You are standing next to what may be the oldest man-made object in Washington not housed in a museum. This stone lantern was carved in 1651 in Edo (now Tokyo), Japan. On 30 March 1954, it was presented to the city to commemorate the centenary of the first Treaty of Peace, Amity and Commerce between the US and Japan, signed by Commodore Matthew Perry. Today, it is lit once a year during the National Cherry Blossom Festival, Washington's annual signal that spring has arrived. The indescribably beautiful display of pink and white blossoms reaches its zenith around the Tidal Basin, where thousands of the trees have been planted since the original gift of two trees was made by the city of Tokyo to the city of Washington in 1912. Just beyond the lantern there is a stone containing a bronze plaque. This marks the site where First Lady Helen Taft and the Japanese ambassador's wife, Viscountess Chinda, planted the first two trees, which still bloom each spring.

NATIONAL CHERRY BLOSSOM FESTIVAL;
www.nationalcherryblossomfestival.org

10 Walk across the Kutz Bridge and proceed until you reach the exit to the Tidal Basin car park. At this point, cross the street and then cross the next one too (Independence Avenue). Turn right and continue along Independence Avenue. Almost immediately, look to your right and left. You will be able to see both the White House and the Thomas Jefferson memorial. Follow Independence Avenue, crossing 15th and then 14th Streets. The next intersection will be 12th Street, SW, where you find yourself back at the starting point of the walk.

ABOVE: MEMORIAL TO GEORGE MASON, THE 18TH-CENTURY VIRGINIAN STATESMAN

A Visit to the Memorial Sites

Disputes and unusual occurrences have repeatedly interrupted the evolution from conception to reality of many of Washington's memorials.

Had you attempted this walk in 1880 or earlier, you would have been wading through the Potomac River. However, in 1881 a flood threatened Washington's city centre and the Army Corps of Engineers began a massive civil-engineering project to create the land that now comprises the western end of the National Mall. The Lincoln memorial was the first to be located here, in 1914. Since then, the placement of memorials along the Reflecting Pool has been steady, though the proceedings have been anything but straightforward. The Washington Monument set the precedent, perhaps, and the proposed site for the National World War II memorial was greeted with strenuous objection. Korean War vets grappled with how their service could be honoured as powerfully as the Vietnam War vets who had, after a wrenching process, finally succeeded in erecting their memorial. Even the revered Abraham Lincoln didn't come by his stately seat at the Mall's terminus easily. This walk takes you to all these sites, and more.

| When exiting Federal Triangle Metro station, follow both sets of escalator steps outside. Proceed straight ahead onto Woodrow Wilson Plaza. Turn left at the silver *Federal Triangle Flowers* sculpture and past the bronze, thumb-like piece *Bearing Witness*, heading out to Constitution Avenue, NW through the arched entryway of the Environmental Protection Agency building. Turn right on Constitution Avenue. Continue and cross 14th Street, NW. At 15th Street, NW cross the street and then follow the path up the small hill to the Washington Monument.

Urban legends abound as to why the marble used to construct the lower portion of this obelisk, in honour of the first US president George Washington (1732–99), looks darker than the stone used for the remainder of the monument. Some have thought it may be caused by floodwater or a result of the US Civil War. However, it is most likely that the responsibility lies with a bizarre political faction called the Know-Nothings, who were the chief suspects in an incident that altered the obelisk's fate. The Washington Monument National Society, which had launched the monument creation as a privately funded project, had made an appeal for building stone as well as financial support. In response to the request, Pope Pius IX offered a block of marble that was originally used to build the Temple of Concord in Rome. On 6 March 1854, the marble disappeared and the Know-Nothings, thought to have anti-Catholic and anti-foreigner sentiments, were accused of stealing the stone. What happened to the marble was unclear – it was either broken into pieces or heaved into the Potomac River – but it was never found and no arrests were made. The incident caused a severe reduction in contributions of both stone and money, and work ground to a halt for 22 years, until 1876. Although the same type of marble was used to complete the construction of the monument, it came from a different quarry and did not weather the same way. Consequently, the stone in the lower portion of the monument is darker than the stone in the upper portion.

THE WASHINGTON MONUMENT;

www.nps.gov/wamo

2 Stand by the Washington Monument, so you can see the Abraham Lincoln memorial straight ahead. Bear to the right, following the path down the hill on which the Monument stands. On your left, just outside the retaining wall, is a short, white column.

If he were alive today, Thomas Jefferson (1743–1826), the third US president, would be pleased to know someone had stopped to acknowledge the Jefferson Pier Stone, which he established in 1804 in order to provide the US with its own prime meridian – one to designate US time as distinct from Greenwich Mean Time. By the mid-19th century, the stone no longer had any function (the meridian of the US was changed to the centre of the Naval Observatory and was later finally subject to Greenwich Mean Time),

OPPOSITE: ABRAHAM LINCOLN, IMMORTALIZED IN MARBLE IN THE LINCOLN MEMORIAL

DISTANCE 2 miles (3.2km)

ALLOW 2 hours

START Federal Triangle Metro station

FINISH Federal Triangle Metro station

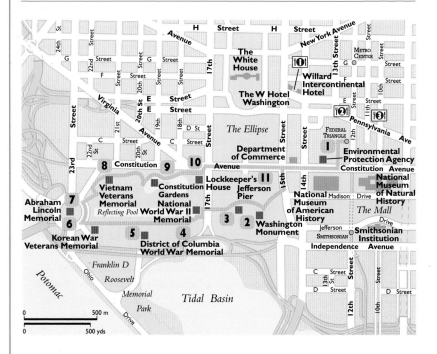

but this spot marks the east–west and north–south axes of the National Mall. Today, it provides an unexpected vista to four Washington landmarks – the White House to the north, the Thomas Jefferson memorial to the south. Look to the west and the Lincoln memorial comes into view; look east to see the US Capitol.

3 Continue along the path until it ends at 17th Street, NW. Cross the street to enter the National World War II memorial.

At the memorial's unveiling on Memorial Day 2004, only a few of the veterans and family members present knew the full extent of the heated debate that had erupted over its placement and design. Many had been enraged by the prospect of a structure blocking the vista from the Lincoln memorial to the Washington Monument. Others insisted that the Mall was already overcrowded with memorials. When architect Friedrich St Florian presented his winning design, some criticized it as echoing the architecture

of the totalitarian regimes US soldiers had fought to defeat; others lamented what they described as warmed-over classicism. In the end, though, the monument did not obstruct the cherished vista, nor did architectural critics universally dismiss it.

NATIONAL WORLD WAR II MEMORIAL;
www.wwiimemorial.com

4 Leave the memorial area, bearing to the left and going past the visitors' information building and toilets. Follow the gravel path parallel to the Reflecting Pool. On your left you will soon see what looks like a white marble temple.

An act of Congress may have authorized the development of the Washington World War I memorial, but it was the citizens themselves, led by newspaperman Frank B. Noyes, who distributed pledge cards and raised the funds. The Doric temple, in honour of veterans of World War I, was designed as a marble bandstand large enough to accommodate the entire Marine Band. John Phillips Sousa himself conducted that band during the unveiling ceremony on Armistice Day in 1931. Subsequent outdoor concerts at the memorial have long ceased.

5 Continue along the gravel path, passing the National Park Service stables. At the end of the path, turn left and walk to the entrance of the Korean War Veterans memorial.

'I wore that type of boots. I carried the radio just like that,' said Bernard Brooks, 62, a Washington resident who served in the Signal Corps during the Korean War. On a sweltering day in July 1995, thousands came to this site to commemorate what is often called the 'forgotten war'. The 19 grim-faced figures encountered here, however, are impossible to forget, particularly at night. Four architects from Pennsylvania State University won the design competition in 1989. They included 38 figures in a column of soldiers moving forwards. Once they realized that their design would have to be altered dramatically to pass review with the various powers that be, they dropped out. They then sued, and lost. Cooper-Lecky Architects of Washington were finally selected for the project, working in tandem with other designers and a veterans' advisory board.

KOREAN WAR VETERANS MEMORIAL;
www.nps.gov/kwvm

ABOVE: THE FIELD OF STARS ON THE FREEDOM WALL AT THE NATIONAL WORLD WAR II MEMORIAL.

6 From the Korean War Veterans memorial, follow the path to the Lincoln memorial.

The construction of this memorial, in honour of the 16th US president Abraham Lincoln (1809–65), began on 12 February 1914, on what would have been his 105th birthday. The public was sceptical, even insulted: the western end of the National Mall was newly created and raw-looking – what kind of tribute would be paid to Lincoln on a site that resembled a wasteland? Seventeen years after the unveiling ceremony in 1922, when black and white audience members had been seated separately, the public had its answer. On Easter Sunday 1939, African-American opera singer Marian Anderson gave a concert on the steps of the memorial that transformed the way many interpreted it, recognizing the part Lincoln had played in the emancipation of slaves (which he achieved in 1863) rather than simply the unifier during the US Civil War. This association of the monument with emancipation and egalitarianism continued to evolve and was crystallized on 28 August 1963, when Martin Luther King delivered his 'I Have a Dream' speech.

LINCOLN MEMORIAL; www.nps.gov/linc

7 Looking across the Reflecting Pool to the Washington Monument, turn left and walk towards the flagpole, which marks the entrance to the Vietnam Veterans memorial.

Little did architecture student Maya Ying Lin know when she entered a design competition sponsored by the Vietnam Veterans Memorial Fund how much her life was about to be transformed. Her entry was the unanimous choice for a Vietnam Veterans memorial in Washington. At the time, she was an undergraduate at Yale University. The black granite wall cut into the earth contains over 50,000 names of soldiers killed and has become one of the most sacred sites in Washington. However, no memorial process has been as fraught with acrimony and misunderstanding: opponents suggested throwing the design out and starting again and the Secretary of the Interior refused to issue a building permit. Finally, the veterans, their supporters and their opponents met to forge a compromise. Lin's powerful black walk of remembrance would remain; representational figures of three servicemen would be added nearby.

8 Follow the path out of the Vietnam Veterans memorial (be sure to look at the Vietnam Women's memorial on your way out). Head towards the pond, bearing to your left and following the path around it until you reach a bridge that crosses over to a small island.

The 56 signatories of the Declaration of Independence are honoured here at the Signers' memorial. This island and pond were unveiled in 1976 as part of the US bicentennial celebration. Ten years later, on the 200th anniversary of the US Constitution, the area was named Constitution Gardens. Look for red-winged blackbirds in the reeds.

9 Leave the island and then follow the path to the stairway. At the top of the stairs, turn left and exit Constitution Gardens onto Constitution Avenue, NW. Turn right and proceed along Constitution Avenue until you see 17th Street, NW.

This stone house, on the southwest corner of 17th Street and Constitution Avenue, is all that remains of a canal that once ran along what is now Constitution Avenue. Erected in 1831, it was the lockkeeper's house at the canal's entrance. Although planned as both functional and decorative, the canal had been lined with timber, making its durability questionable. By the time of the US Civil War (1861–65), the canal had become a garbage-strewn, fetid eyesore. It was filled in and turned into a street soon after the war.

10 Follow Constitution Avenue for two more blocks. Make sure to look to your left for a view of the White House between 17th and 15th Streets. After you cross 14th Street, start to notice the detailed sculpture on the Environmental Protection Agency Building on the left.

In the 1930s, funding was given to adorn these government headquarters with exterior sculpture. Five ornamental panels feature on the Constitution Avenue side of the buildings. Above the entrance, near 14th Street, a woman represents *Abundance and Industry*, while two rams represent *Productivity and Security*; a vase pours forth the *Fruits of Industry*. A

WHERE TO EAT

🍽 CAFÉ DU PARC,
1401 Pennsylvania Avenue, NW;
Tel: 1-202-942-7000.
Charming bistro for breakfast, lunch and dinner; ground-floor cafe. $$

🍽 LES HALLES,
1201 Pennsylvania Avenue, NW;
Tel: 1-202-347-6848.
Steak frîtes, mussels and other brasserie standbys; patio. $$

🍽 TEN PENH,
1001 Pennsylvania Avenue, NW;
Tel: 1-202-393-4500.
A very popular restaurant serving Asian-style cuisine. $$$

little further along the avenue you can see *Labor and Industry,* represented by a male figure and a bull accompanied by a sheaf of wheat and a millstone. The remaining panels are *Columbia* (in the centre), *Commerce and Communications* and *Interstate Transportation*. Notice the frieze that extends the length of the complex, consisting of a wild variety of human, animal and other forms. As you approach 12th Street, NW notice the bas-relief over the entrance to the Andrew Mellon Auditorium. It depicts Lieutenant General George Washington planning the Battle of Trenton, New Jersey.

11 To return to Federal Triangle Metro station, turn left on 12th Street.

GRIM-FACED SOLDIERS OF THE UNFORGETTABLE KOREAN WAR VETERANS MEMORIAL

A Walk along America's Grand Avenue

A promenade along Washington's grandest avenue and, arguably, the most famous street in the US should not be missed.

Pennsylvania Avenue is the all-important mile linking the White House to the US Capitol. It is thought the street's name was intended to smooth the ruffled feathers of Pennsylvanian politicians, who considered Philadelphia a more suitable locale for the nation's capital. Ever since Thomas Jefferson walked down Pennsylvania Avenue for his inauguration in 1801, it has witnessed countless parades, marches and demonstrations. Depending on the time of day you choose for your stroll, Pennsylvania Avenue will either bustle with activity – its extra-wide pavements crowded with pedestrians – or appear all but deserted, its grand edifices like slumbering giants, still and shuttered. It's then that you notice the different eras of Washington history reflected along this grand boulevard. Evidence of what was probably its most fascinating time – from the city's founding in 1791 up to the US Civil War years (1861–65) – is sadly gone. However, the late 19th and 20th centuries are well represented, waiting to be appreciated on foot.

When exiting Federal Triangle Metro station, follow both sets of escalator steps outside. Proceed straight ahead onto Woodrow Wilson Plaza. Turn right at the silver *Federal Triangle Flowers* sculpture, heading out to Pennsylvania Avenue, NW. Turn left. On the corner of Pennsylvania Avenue and 14th Street, NW is the John Wilson Building.

The offices of Washington's mayor and city council are housed in this 1908 building. Prior to that, a large powerhouse for the electric trams that ran up and down 14th Street was located here. Supposedly constructed to be fireproof, the powerhouse nonetheless burned down in one hour flat during a devastating fire. Ironically, the only wall remaining bore a sign that read, 'Absolutely Fireproof'. The statue outside the main entrance of the John Wilson Building is of Alexander R. 'Boss' Shepherd, who headed a massive public works campaign in 1871, after the city of Washington was granted its first opportunity at self-governance. However, Shepherd's corrupt policies led to the removal of this privilege.

2 Cross 14th Street and then Pennsylvania Avenue. Walk one block past the park on the left. At the intersection of 14th and E Streets, NW is the Willard Hotel.

This is the last example of the grand and luxurious hotels that once lined Pennsylvania Avenue. In 1901, hotelier Henry Willard razed his original property to construct this lavish replacement, but

WHERE TO EAT

🍴 701,
701 Pennsylvania Avenue, NW;
Tel: 1-202-393-0701.
Contemporary continental cuisine and live jazz in the evening. $$$

🍴 THE OCCIDENTAL,
1475 Pennsylvania Avenue, NW;
Tel: 1-202-783-1475.
Known for fine dining since 1906; outdoor seating. $$$

🍴 W HOTEL ROOF TERRACE,
15th and Pennsylvania Avenue, NW,
Tel: 1-202-661-2400.
Hip bar; views of the White House and Washington Monument. $$$

financial difficulties nearly caused it to face the demolition ball in the late 1960s/early 1970s. After being boarded up for 18 years, the decaying lobby and public spaces were completely restored, and the hotel reopened in 1986. Take a look inside and see the results for yourself. Make sure to visit the Willard's Hall of History located just inside the F Street entrance, then order a Mint Julep from the Round Robin Bar.

3 Cross 14th Street, turn right and cross E Street. Step up onto Freedom Plaza.

Freedom Plaza, designed by architect Robert Venturi in 1980, is named in honour of Martin Luther King (1929–68),

OPPOSITE: ORNATE LOBBY OF THE WILLARD HOTEL ON PENNSYLVANIA AVENUE

DISTANCE 1.5 miles (2.5km)

ALLOW 1 hour (more with site visits)

START Federal Triangle Metro station

FINISH Archives-Navy Memorial-Penn Quarter Metro station

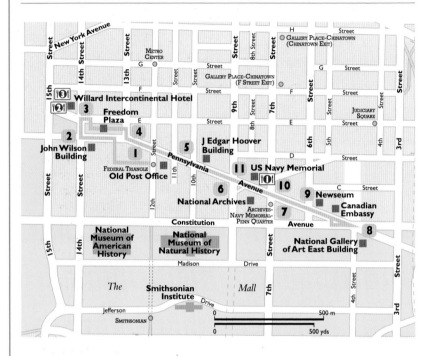

who finished work on his famous 'I Have a Dream' speech at the Willard Hotel in 1963. As you walk across it, notice the inlaid rendering of the central part of the city plan of Washington, which was designed by French-born American architect, engineer and urban designer Pierre Charles L'Enfant (1754–1825) in 1791. Around the city plan, there are quotes about Washington from famous people carved into the paving. Venturi had originally proposed tall, stone pylons and large-scale models of the White

House and Capitol, but these were never built. The plaza is a popular venue for outdoor concerts, rallies and, unofficially, skateboarders. A time capsule, which contains the slain civil-rights leader's robe, Bible and other memorabilia, is buried here and is scheduled to be opened 15 January 2088.

4 Walk across Freedom Plaza, then cross 13th Street. Continue on Pennsylvania Avenue to the intersection of 12th to the Old Post Office building.

Pennsylvania Avenue was the city's first commercial thoroughfare, lined with shops, markets and a financial district. By the end of the 19th century, however, the corridor had begun to decline. In an attempt to improve its prospects, Congress authorized construction of a combined Post Office Department headquarters and City Post Office building. In 1899, this striking Romanesque Revival building was completed, its clock tower, 315ft (96m) high, becoming an instant landmark – you can still take a lift to the top. The Post Office Department left in 1930 and the threat of demolition loomed over the building. Finally, in the early 1980s, a group of preservationists persisted in having it restored. Moreover, their campaign, known as 'Don't Tear It Down' grew into the DC Preservation League, which continues to carry the flag for preserving the city's buildings.

OLD POST OFFICE TOWER;

SUMMER: MON–FRI 9–7.45, SAT–SUN 10–5.45; WINTER: MON–FRI 9–4.45, SAT–SUN 10–5.45; www.nps.gov/opot

5 Walk down Pennsylvania Avenue. The buildings on the south side of the street are located within the Federal Triangle, an enormous construction project undertaken by the federal government in 1926. Its goal was to reclaim what in the 19th century had been the city's seamy Red Light District for a triangular-shaped precinct of government headquarters. The six limestone buildings with red-tiled roofs are the result. At the intersection of Pennsylvania Avenue and 10th Street, NW is a building from a different era, the J. Edgar Hoover Building.

The Federal Bureau of Investigation has been headquartered in this imposing, impenetrable fortress since 1974. US lawyer John Edgar Hoover (1895–1972), the building's namesake, was director of the Bureau for 48 years. Highly regarded while he was alive, various allegations tarnished Hoover's reputation after his death. His leadership spanned a staggering eight presidential administrations, encompassing Prohibition, the Great

Depression, World War II, the Korean War, the Cold War and the Vietnam War. Especially during the 1960s, Hoover was accused of exceeding and abusing his authority, investigating individuals and groups because of their political beliefs rather than suspected criminal activity. It is because of Hoover's long and controversial reign that FBI directors are now limited to 10-year terms.

6 Cross 9th Street, NW and then turn right and cross Pennsylvania Avenue. Look for a stone tablet near the corner of 9th Street and Pennsylvania Avenue.

In 1941, President Franklin D. Roosevelt (1882–1945) met with his friend Supreme Court Justice Felix Frankfurter in his office. Roosevelt told Frankfurter, 'If they are to put any memorial to me, I should like it to be placed in the centre of that green plot in front of the Archives building. I should like it to consist of a block about the size of this' (meaning his desk). In 1965, Roosevelt's request was granted. Thirty-two years later, a second $48 million Franklin D. Roosevelt memorial was unveiled at the Tidal Basin (see Walk 3). Inside the National Archives, visitors can view the original Declaration of Independence, US Constitution and Bill of Rights. The building was designed by architect John Russell Pope (1874–1937) and opened in 1935.

NATIONAL ARCHIVES;
SPRING AND SUMMER: DAILY 10–7; AUTUMN AND WINTER: DAILY 10–5.30;
www.archives.gov/nae/visit

7 Cross Pennsylvania Avenue at 7th Street, NW. Continue past the building situated at the tip of the Federal Triangle: the Federal Trade Commission. Cross 6th Street, NW, passing the National Gallery of Art West Building on the right. Across 4th Street, NW is the National Gallery's East Building.

In a city of conservative, classically derived structures, the National Gallery's East Building is a breath of fresh air. Designed by famed Chinese-born US architect, I.M. Pei (born 1917), historians and critics widely regard it as the best example of modern architecture in the US capital city. Rising gracefully from an awkward trapezoidal site, the building is divided into two triangles – one for gallery space, the other for offices. Even if you don't have time to look around the gallery, it's worth a look inside just to experience Pei's solution first hand – standing beneath the light-filled atrium, with a large mobile by Alexander Calder peacefully turning overhead, is a pleasure in itself. Funding for the gallery, which opened in 1978, was given by Paul Mellon and Ailsa Mellon Bruce, son and daughter of the National Gallery's founder, Andrew Mellon.

NATIONAL GALLERY OF ART;
MON–SAT 10–5, SUN 11–6;
www.nga.gov

8 Outside the East Building, cross Constitution Avenue, NW and turn left, returning to Pennsylvania Avenue. Pass John Marshall Park on the right, to arrive at the Canadian Embassy.

The embassies of the two countries that border the US – Canada and Mexico – sit on Pennsylvania Avenue. (Mexico's can be found on the stretch between the White House and Georgetown.) Architectural elements of the Canadian Embassy, designed by Vancouver-based architect Arthur Erickson (born 1924), pay tribute to neighbouring buildings: the exterior of the embassy is sheathed in white marble; the rotunda echoes those of the Capitol and National Gallery West Building; and the building's three wings are positioned to reflect the geometric minimalism of the National Gallery East Building. At the end of the 19th century, this block of Pennsylvania Avenue was the heart of Washington's original Chinatown. However, in 1931 the community was forced to relocate to its current site along H Street, NW to make way for the construction of a municipal centre. Years later, in the mid 1980s, a portion of that new Chinatown was displaced for the construction of the Washington Convention Center.

9 Next door to the embassy is the Newseum.

When it opened in April 2008, the Newseum injected a rare boost of technological pizzazz and curatorial bravura along what has traditionally been a fairly refined block of Pennsylvania Avenue. When you've finished with the exhibits, which cover five centuries of news history, the view of Pennsylvania Avenue and the National Mall from the observation deck is incomparable.

10 Continue along Pennsylvania Avenue, crossing 6th Street and then 7th Street, NW. In the middle of the block is the US Navy memorial.

The US Navy memorial and the Market Square development on its border were constructed between 1984 and 1990. Preservationists objected when 8th Street, NW was closed off for the memorial, opposing the alteration to the original city plan conceived by Pierre Charles L'Enfant in 1791. Yet the memorial's plaza does at least retain the vista from the avenue to the majestic former Patent Office Building to the north. The former Patent Office Building and the National Archives are the focal points for what has become the best public outdoor space along Pennsylvania Avenue.

11 The Metro station is adjacent to the Navy Memorial.

43

Great Estates of Georgetown

Impressive mansions and gardens are featured on this walk that introduces you to some of the most historic properties in Washington.

One of the most remarkable aspects of the Georgetown historic district is that it represents a complete town, with commercial, residential and civic buildings still intact. In a densely developed city like Washington, visitors are amazed to discover four Georgetown estates that have retained much of their original acreage. They are located high above the waterfront and bustling commercial corridor on terrain that follows the slope and rise of the old road, where workers used to roll casks of tobacco from rural Maryland down to the inspection station on the banks of the Potomac. The prosperous merchants whose fortunes were made in the tobacco trade built large, freestanding Federal-style houses (1790–1820) along Prospect and N Streets. Further north, however, other wealthy Georgetown families such as the Davidsons and the Peters created expansive estates featuring grand mansions and landscaped gardens. These manorial houses are the subject of this walk. Try to take it Tuesday to Saturday, when the houses are open for tours.

Leaving Dupont Circle Metro, turn left onto Q Street, NW and follow it two blocks to Massachusetts Avenue, NW. Cross Massachusetts Avenue and continue on Q Street until you reach the entrance to the Dumbarton Bridge (known as the Buffalo Bridge for the massive animals guarding the approach). Cross the bridge over the Rock Creek as you enter Georgetown. Make sure to look to your right about halfway across for a view to the Washington National Cathedral. Follow Q Street, NW until you arrive at Dumbarton House at No. 2715.

Dumbarton House stands on a tract of land patented in 1703 by an immigrant Scot, Ninian Beall, who named it 'Rock of Dumbarton'. In 1798, a developer bought 4.5 acres (1.8 hectares) of the land and began to construct the house. The First Lady Dolley Madison stayed overnight in the house following the burning of the White House in the War of 1812. When the Dumbarton Bridge was constructed in 1915, the house faced possible demolition, so preservationists had it moved 100ft (30m) to its present site, thus allowing the extension of Q Street into Georgetown. The primly named National Society of The Colonial Dames of America purchased the home in 1928, restored it to its early Federal period character, and bestowed the present name of Dumbarton House. Tours include the music room, parlour and upstairs bedrooms, where visitors can see a wealth of furniture, paintings, textiles, silver and ceramics that were made and used in America's early years.

DUMBARTON HOUSE;
TUE–SAT (TOURS 10.15, 11.15, 12.15, 1.15);
www.dumbartonhouse.org

2 Follow Q Street to 28th Street, NW, then turn right and begin to walk up the hill. When you are about halfway, stop outside the street entrance to No. 1628 28th Street.

Evermay is the last privately owned estate in Georgetown. The house is not open to the public unless you are invited to a party or reception. Built in 1801, its original owner was Samuel Davidson, a Scottish immigrant who made a fortune in real estate. That privacy was of utmost importance to him can be gleaned from the inscription on the bronze plaque that hangs on the 28th Street wall. He begs his neighbours to avoid Evermay 'as they would a den of evils, or rattlesnakes, and thereby save themselves and me much

DISTANCE 3 miles (4.8km)

ALLOW 2.5 hours (or more with museum visits)

START Dupont Circle Metro station (Q Street exit)

FINISH Foggy Bottom Metro station

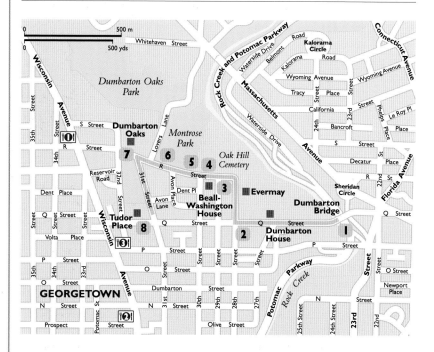

vexation and trouble'. This warning was issued via a newspaper advertisement placed by Davidson. When he died, the residence went to his nephew, Lewis Grant, with the proviso that he emigrate from Scotland and add 'Davidson' to his name. Grant complied and lived out his life on the estate.

3 Proceed on 28th Street, following as it curves into R Street, NW past a cemetery. Cross R Street at 29th Street, NW and stand in front of 2029 R Street.

On 23 July 2001, friends, family and admirers of Katharine Graham, who had died at age 84, repaired to this house (built in 1784) for a reception following her funeral at the Washington National Cathedral. They paid tribute to a woman who had surprised herself when, inexperienced and uncertain, she took over control of the *Washington Post* newspaper following the suicide of her husband. During her tenure the *Post* rose to prominence and Graham became one of the most influential and admired

women of her generation. She was at the helm of the newspaper when it made history with the publication of the *Pentagon Papers* during the Vietnam War and again when two *Post* reporters broke the story that became Watergate and resulted in the resignation of President Richard Nixon. In 1997, Graham published her memoir, *Personal History*, which received critical acclaim, became a bestseller and won the Pulitzer Prize for biography. With her death, a glittering era for Georgetown social and political life came to an end.

4 Cross R Street and walk to the entry gate of Oak Hill Cemetery.

Picturesque Oak Hill Cemetery descends from R Street to the Rock Creek Parkway below via a series of ravines and alternating terraces. Established in 1849, it takes its name from the grove of huge oak trees that provided shade for those who brought picnics here to commune both with nature and their deceased loved ones. The charming Gothic Revival chapel, built in 1850, was designed by Smithsonian Castle architect James Renwick (1818–95). Look for the simple gravestone of Katharine Graham, owner and publisher of the *Washington Post*, on the chapel grounds. Other notables laid to rest here are statesman Edwin M. Stanton (1814–69), Secretary of War under President Abraham Lincoln; architect Adolph Cluss (1825–1905); socialite Peggy O'Neale Eaton (1799–1879), whose marriage to President Andrew Jackson's Secretary of War split the Cabinet in two, and William W. Corcoran (1798–1888), the banker and philanthropist who donated the land for the cemetery.

OAK HILL CEMETERY;
MON–FRI 9–4.30, SUN 1–4;
www.oakhillcemeterydc.org

5 Next to Oak Hill Cemetery is the lovely, rural Montrose Park.

A favourite spot for dog walkers and youngsters with a nanny or parent in tow, Montrose Park was once the site of a mansion by that name built here in 1810. Make sure to read the sign that tells you all about the Parrott rope walk, an operation that took place when rope-making magnate, Richard Parrott, owned the land. Sarah Louisa Rittenhouse, a Georgetown native who had grown up at Dumbarton House, campaigned to turn the acreage into a park. In 1911, the decaying Montrose mansion was razed and a new National Park welcomed the public. To honour Rittenhouse's accomplishment, in 1956 the Georgetown Garden Club placed a bronze armillary sphere near the park's entrance. She is buried in Oak Hill Cemetery.

6 Continue along R Street past Lovers Lane, a path down to Rock Creek Park that separates Montrose Park from the more formal gardens of Dumbarton Oaks at 31st and R Streets, NW.

This estate dates back to 1801, although it would be difficult to tell from looking at the house, which has been altered extensively. The land was part of the 'Rock of Dumbarton' tract owned by Ninian Beall. The original mansion was later transformed by another owner into a fashionable house in the style of the Second Empire (1850–80). In 1920, Robert and Mildred Bliss purchased the property and renovated extensively, stripping away the Second Empire elements. They also enlisted landscape architect Beatrix Farrand to create a formal garden for the estate, a stroll through which should not be missed.

ABOVE: DUMBARTON OAKS, WITH ITS ORNATE PAVED COURTYARD

When they moved to California in 1940, the Blisses gave the bulk of Dumbarton Oaks to Harvard University, which in 1963 commissioned architect Philip Johnson to design the Pre-Columbian Museum, where the Bliss's collection is now on display.

DUMBARTON OAKS;

15 MARCH–31 OCTOBER: TUE–SUN 2–6; 1 NOVEMBER–14 MARCH: TUE–SUN 2–5; www.doaks.org

7 From Dumbarton Oaks, cross R Street and proceed along 31st Street, NW. Enjoy the splendid brick and clapboard homes you pass before you reach the entrance of Tudor Place, which will be on your right.

Six generations of the Peter family lived here continuously between 1805 and 1983. Their ownership began when Thomas and Martha Custis Peter bought an unfinished house that stood on this site. Martha was the granddaughter of First Lady Martha Washington and her husband was the son of Georgetown's first mayor. They hired William Thornton, first architect of the US Capitol, to complete the house, which he did in 1816. Many consider the finished product to be not only Thornton's masterpiece, but also one of the most important houses in Washington for providing insight into domestic life in the city's first two centuries. The Peters bore witness to such important events as the laying of the US Capitol cornerstone, the burning of Washington in 1814, and the US Civil War. This is one of the best,

WHERE TO EAT

🍽 BISTRO LEPIC,
1736 Wisconsin Avenue, NW;
Tel: 1-202-333-0111.
A perennial favourite with locals, serving classic French bistro fare downstairs; wine bar upstairs. $$

🍽 MARTIN'S TAVERN,
1264 Wisconsin Avenue, NW;
Tel: 1-202-333-7370.
Traditional American food with a British streak. $$

🍽 MARVELOUS MARKET,
3217 P Street, NW;
Tel: 1-202-333-2591.
One of Washington's best takeaways, with award-winning chocolate chip cookies. $

and most beautiful, places to learn about Georgetown life during the 19th century.

TUDOR PLACE;

TUE–SAT 10–4, SUN 12–4 (CLOSED JANUARY); www.tudorplace.org

8 To get to Foggy Bottom Metro station, turn right at the exit of Tudor Place grounds and walk downhill on 31st Street to M Street, NW. Turn left onto M Street and follow it to the intersection of 28th Street, NW. Turn right, crossing M Street, and then turn right and proceed along Pennsylvania Avenue, NW. Follow Pennsylvania Avenue to 23rd Street, NW. Turn right onto 23rd Street. The station is on the right.

Scandals in the Presidents' Back Yard

The 7-acre (2.8-hectare) park north of the White House has been the site of some of Washington's most infamous machinations.

'La Fayette Square was society,' wrote novelist, journalist and Washington resident Henry Adams (1838–1918) '…One found all one's acquaintances as well as hotels, banks, markets, and national government. Beyond the Square the country began'. And what about inside the Square? That's another story, and one that Adams chronicled in 1880 with his anonymously published *Democracy*, a novel about political power – its acquisition, use and abuse set in the elegant enclave of Lafayette Square. It afforded its inhabitants proximity to power and social cachet. It also spawned a remarkable number of scandalous events, a selection of which is introduced on this walk. There's the senator who pioneered the modern political campaign; a suicide that's followed by cold-blooded murder; and the president who refuses to be intimidated by assassins. And let us not forget the secretary who shredded and smuggled top-secret documents. Take the walk on a weekday, when the government offices surrounding the park are in full swing.

1 Exiting McPherson Square Metro station at Vermont Avenue, NW, turn right and walk one block to H Street, NW. Cross H Street and continue along Madison Place, NW to the second yellow house on the left – the one with the wrought-iron balcony.

Benjamin Tayloe, who was a member of one of the wealthiest families in Virginia, built this house in 1828 and lived there for 40 years, keeping a journal of his residency published as *Our Neighbors on Lafayette Square*. It's a pity that he did not live long enough to record events here between 1900 and 1902, when the home was leased by Senator Mark Hanna of Ohio and became known as the Little White House. Hanna was a wealthy industrialist who many believed exerted great influence over Ohio governor William McKinley. As chairman of the Republican National Committee, Hanna promoted McKinley as his party's 1896 presidential candidate. He personally took charge of the campaign, raising an unprecedented $3.5 million, employing 1,400 people, and outspending his opponent, William Jennings Bryan, by 12 to 1. It is considered the forerunner of the modern political campaign. McKinley won the election, and Hanna's close relationship with the now President continued, McKinley partaking in countless 'power breakfasts' at this house in order to confer with Hanna.

2 Next door to the Tayloe House is the entrance to the US Court of Claims and Court of Appeals. Walk up the steps and into the courtyard. On the wall at the far right is a large plaque illustrating the Rodgers House.

Although the assassination of President Abraham Lincoln is one of the most well-known events in US history, what is less known is the scope of the plot hatched by Lincoln's murderer, John Wilkes Booth. His intention was to kill not only the President but to assassinate General Ulysses Grant, Vice President Andrew Johnson and Secretary of State William Seward on the same night. Seward rented the house that once stood on this site while he served as secretary of state. It was here, on 14 April 1865, that he was brutally attacked by would-be assassin Lewis Powell, assigned by Booth to 'slit the throat of the old man'. Powell had entered the house claiming to be a messenger bringing a prescription for Seward, who was recovering from a carriage accident; his attack wounded the secretary of state yet did not kill him. It was Powell, in fact, who would suffer death after being arrested, found guilty and sentenced to death by hanging. Seward recovered from knife wounds that had been inflicted by Powell, as did two of his sons who had also been injured. However, it was all too much for Seward's wife Frances, who died two months later of a heart attack.

3 Return to Madison Place and follow it to the intersection of Pennsylvania Avenue, NW. Turn right, cross Madison Place and stand in front of the sculpture group on the corner.

OPPOSITE: THE HAY-ADAMS HOTEL

DISTANCE 0.5 mile (0.8km)

ALLOW I hour

START McPherson Square Metro station (Vermont Avenue exit)

FINISH McPherson Square Metro station (Vermont Avenue entrance)

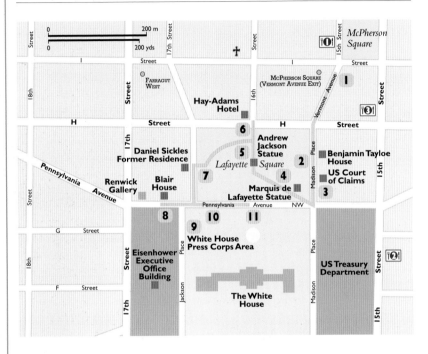

For two weeks in 1824, Washington was abuzz over the arrival of the Marquis de Lafayette (1757–1834), who is depicted atop the pedestal. Congress had finally seen fit to landscape President's Park, as this 7 acres (2.8 hectares) was originally known, because the Marquis – a French military officer and beloved hero to the American public for his service to the US military during the American War of Independence – was due to give a speech here. Following the ceremony, the park was popularly called Lafayette Park or Lafayette Square. Three other foreign-born military men are honoured on the other corners of the park, each having rendered service to the US during the American War of Independence (1775–83).

4 Follow the path from the Lafayette statue into the centre of the park. There you will find the first equestrian statue ever erected in America. It commemorates General Andrew Jackson.

OPPOSITE: FIRST EQUESTRIAN STATUE IN THE US, COMMEMORATING GENERAL ANDREW JACKSON

In 1853, to much fanfare, General Andrew Jackson (1767–1845), triumphant at the Battles of New Orleans and Pensacola during the War of 1812, was honoured with the unveiling of this statue. Jackson later served as America's seventh president (the first ever Democratic president). His inaugural reception is famous for its raucous nature, with thousands roaming through the White House and causing extensive damage. The only means of getting the crowd to leave was to drag tubs of rum punch out onto Lafayette Square.

5 Walk around the Jackson statue to the other side and continue to H Street. Cross H Street to 16th Street, NW. On the left side is the Hay-Adams Hotel.

The hotel is named after the owners of the homes that once occupied this site. The Hay and Adams families built two magnificent mansions designed by US architect Henry Hobson Richardson. However, they were razed in 1926 to make way for the hotel. The owners of the 16th Street house were John and Clara Hay; the H Street residence belonged to Henry and Marion 'Clover' Adams. However, Clover never lived in the house. On 6 December 1885 she took her own life by ingesting potassium cyanide, dying on her bedroom floor in the Adams' rented house one block away. She and her husband were two of the most illustrious and enigmatic residents of Lafayette Square and their Boston Brahmin lineage, keen intelligence and exclusive social circle were of unending interest to their neighbours. A few unsympathetic types placed the blame for Clover's death at Henry Adams' feet, although nothing has ever come from such speculation. In fact, letters written by Clover to her sister Ellen would indicate that Henry regarded his wife with tenderness. An air of mystery continues to hover over the suicide of Mrs Adams nonetheless, many seeking answers at the powerful memorial placed on Clover's gravesite in Rock Creek Cemetery. A copy of the statue depicting an androgynous cloaked figure can actually be seen inside the Court of Claims courtyard on the left side.

6 Cross H Street back to Lafayette Park. Turn right and walk along the path that leads through the park to the other side. Cross Jackson Place, NW and find No. 722 along the terrace.

Today, almost all of the buildings in this terrace accommodate White House offices. However, many were once private residences. A house that once stood on the site of No. 722 was once the scene of a Washington scandal. Congressman Daniel E. Sickles and his young wife, Teresa, lived at this address. In February 1859, an anonymous letter sent to Sickles stated that his wife was engaged in an illicit relationship with his friend Mr Philip Barton Key, son of the man who wrote the lyrics to the US national anthem. 'He has as much use of your wife as you do', the letter declared. Sickles became enraged. Although himself unfaithful to the bonds of marriage, this dual betrayal by his wife and by a man he considered his trusted friend was intolerable. Three days later, upon seeing Barton Key attempt to signal to Teresa across Lafayette Square, Sickles burst through the front door of his Jackson Place house, stormed across the park and shot at Barton Key three times. The hapless suitor died soon after, and Sickles gave himself up to the law. The resulting trial was a national sensation, particularly when the verdict was given against the congressman: not guilty due to temporary insanity, the first time such a defence had been used successfully in the US.

7 Looking at No. 722 turn left and follow Jackson Place to Pennsylvania Avenue. Turn right and proceed to 1651 Pennsylvania Avenue, called Blair House – the building with the green awning extending from the entrance.

While renovations were carried out at the White House between 1947 and 1951, President Harry Truman and his wife, Bess, moved out temporarily to Blair House. On 1 November 1950, two Puerto Rican nationalists began to shoot their way inside the building, determined to assassinate the president. A quick response by the White House police prevented their plan from being carried out, yet one officer, Leslie Coffelt, was killed. The plaque closest to the entry gate pays tribute to him. Security for President Truman became tighter, although Truman did not understand all the fuss. To the alarm of the Secret Service, he had stuck his head out of the second-floor window

WHERE TO EAT

🍴 **GEORGIA BROWN'S,**
950 15th Street, NW;
Tel: 1-202-393-4499.
Upscale southern cooking at its best. The Sunday brunch is bountiful. **$$**

🍴 **OLD EBBITT GRILL,**
675 15th Street, NW;
Tel: 1-202-347-4800.
Voted 'best place to talk politics', this restaurant has an American menu for plain and fancy tastes. **$$**

🍴 **LE BAR,**
Sofitel Lafayette Square;
806 15th Street, NW;
Tel: 1-202-730-8700.
A chic urban setting featuring light French fare. Popular for after-work drinks on the outdoor patio. **$$**

of Blair House during the attack to see what was going on. Later, he wrote to a friend, 'I've been shot at by experts and unless your name's on the bullet you needn't be afraid'. Today, Blair House serves as guest quarters for visiting heads of state who are in Washington for an official meeting with the US president.

8 Cross Pennsylvania Avenue and stand in front of the grandiose Eisenhower Executive Office Building.

The original occupants of this massive building, built in the Second Empire style (popular in the US between 1850

and 1880) were the State, Navy and War Departments. When they all moved to new headquarters, every inch of space inside became White House offices. A secretary named Fawn Hall worked in room 392. It was notorious in the late 1980s for the 'shredding parties', where secret documents were destroyed. Hall's superior was Lieutenant Colonel Oliver North, a notable figure in the Iran-Contra scandal, which involved arms sales to Iran and funding of Contra militants in Nicaragua. How ironic that Hall's smuggling of confidential papers out of her employer's office caused President Ronald Reagan to form a task force that eventually put both North and Hall on trial. In March 1989, having been granted immunity in exchange for her testimony, Hall testified against North. She told of shredding documents, at one point claiming, 'Sometimes you have to go above the law'.

9 Facing the Executive Office Building, turn left and walk past the entry gate to the White House grounds. Just past the fence is an area filled with camera equipment.

Located just outside the White House's West Wing lobby and press briefing room, television correspondents use this area for 'stand-ups' while they report the news of White House scandals. Constant use over the years caused the spot to become muddy and grass refused to grow, so, in 1998, the White House installed honeycomb grating and gravel to create what is known as Pebble Beach.

10 Continue along Pennsylvania Avenue until you are standing looking at the White House.

This famous edifice has witnessed many a reputation tarnished by scandal. A handful of occupants have suffered the ignominy of being removed from office. The process begins with impeachment, in which a public official is accused of wrong-doing by the House of Representatives. Next comes a trial by the Senate, after which a president can be forced out of office. Andrew Johnson (17th US president 1865–69) was the first president to leave office as a result of impeachment. In the wake of the Watergate debacle, President Richard Nixon, who had been president since 1969, avoided impeachment by resigning in 1974. Former White House intern Monica Lewinsky, who told a confidante about her affair with Bill Clinton (president 1993–2001), caused a storm of gossip and legal prosecution that resulted in a graphic 453-page report to Congress, providing details of the intern's hopes, dreams and sexual proclivities. Bill Clinton soon became the second US president to be impeached. However, the charges of perjury and obstruction of justice ended with his acquittal.

11 To get back to the Metro, cross Lafayette Park, past the Andrew Jackson statue, back to H Street. Turn right and proceed to the intersection of H Street and Vermont Avenue. Cross H Street and follow Vermont Avenue one block. The station will be on the left.

OPPOSITE: THE EISENHOWER EXECUTIVE OFFICE BUILDING, AN EXAMPLE OF SECOND EMPIRE ARCHITECTURE

A Walk through the Corridors of Power

The US Capitol represents the heart of America's democratic government and the geographic centre of Washington.

This walk leads you around Washington's most famous architectural icon, the US Capitol, and past the buildings housing America's legislative and judicial branches of government. You will discover that Capitol Hill does indeed describe a rise in the ground upon which the monumental edifice stands. Take this walk during the working week, when the streets are filled with members of Congress and their staff. You'll notice impromptu conferences being held on street corners and advice being hastily conveyed via mobile phones. Sleek black town cars and humble city taxis will pick up and drop off lobbyists eager to pitch their cause. It may come as a surprise that such intensive activity takes place amidst a gracious park-like setting, the US Capitol grounds representing some of the most pleasing outdoor spaces in the city. Pay attention to the street signs, too: the Capitol marks the spot from which the principal streets separating Washington's four main areas radiate. You will walk through each of them.

1 Directly across 1st Street, SE from the Capitol South Metro station is the Capitol Hill Club at No. 300.

The concept of a national social club for Republicans was first proposed by New Jersey Congressman James C. Auchincloss in 1950. The organization has occupied this site since 1972. Presidents, vice presidents, members of Congress, governors and state party leaders are among the members who enjoy meals in the Presidential Dining Room or drinks at the Auchincloss Grill. The National Democratic Club can be found nearby on Ivy Street, SE.

MAJESTY OF LAW

2 Looking at the Capitol Hill Club, turn left and continue on 1st Street, crossing C Street, SE. At Independence Avenue, SE, turn left. Pass the Cannon and Longworth House Office Buildings. Next is the Rayburn House Office Building on the left. Each of these buildings contains offices for members of the House of Representatives.

The Rayburn Building was named in honour of Sam T. Rayburn of Texas, a lifelong bachelor and member of the United States House of Representatives from 1913 until his death in 1961. He served as Speaker of the House (leader of the House of Representatives) for 17 years and is regarded as the most effective Speaker in history. In shaping legislation, Rayburn preferred to work quietly in the background rather than be in the public spotlight. As Speaker, he won a reputation for fairness and integrity, refusing to accept gifts or money from lobbyists. His legendary after-hours 'Board of Education' meetings, held in hideaway offices in the House, were off-the-record sessions where invitees of Rayburn would play poker, sip bourbon and engage in frank political discussion. An invitation to attend was considered a high honour.

3 Continue along Independence Avenue. At the intersection of 1st Street, SW turn right and cross Independence Avenue. Turn left onto Maryland Avenue, SW and look for the entrance to the US Botanic Garden.

Sited here since 1933, this is the offspring of earlier botanic gardens established by Congress. It includes a conservatory, 2 acres (0.8 hectares) of surrounding grounds, as well as a garden across

OPPOSITE: GRANT MEMORIAL; ABOVE: STATUE IN FRONT OF THE RAYBURN HOUSE OFFICE BUILDING

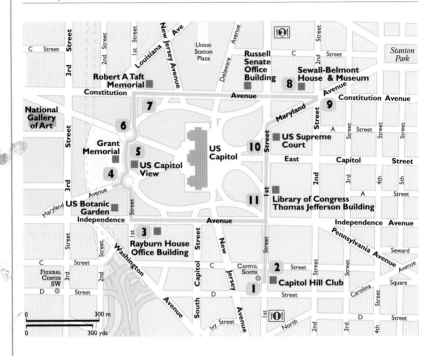

DISTANCE 0.7 mile (1.2km)

ALLOW I hour (more with site visits)

START Capitol South Metro station

FINISH Capitol South Metro station

Independence Avenue displaying the
Frédéric Auguste Bartholdi Fountain,
which commemorates the French
sculptor (1834–1904) who created the
Statue of Liberty. Always an inviting
refuge from the demands of Capitol
Hill, the Botanic Garden is especially
welcoming on a frosty winter's day.
US BOTANIC GARDEN;
DAILY 10–5; www.usbg.gov

4 Follow Maryland Avenue back to
1st Street and turn left. Almost

immediately on your right will be a
stunning view of the west terrace of
the US Capitol.

Undoubtedly one of the most recognized
buildings in the world, the US Capitol
has stood on this hillside since the federal
government located to Washington in
1800. Beneath its massive cast-iron dome,
members of Congress go about their
work, which is chiefly to make laws. The
body is required to assemble once every
year at noon on the third day of January.

A Congress lasts two years and is divided into two sessions. The Senate is composed of 100 members, two from each state; the House of Representatives has 435 members, elected every two years from each of the 50 states apportioned to their total populations. The Commonwealth of Puerto Rico, the District of Columbia and US Territories all have representatives. Take note, however, that although these delegates enjoy most of the prerogatives of representatives, they do not have the right to vote on matters before the House. This reality continues to infuriate Washington citizens, who addressed the matter by revising the District licence plate design to read: 'Taxation Without Representation'.

US CAPITOL GUIDE SERVICE;
MON–SAT 9–4; TEL: 1-202-225-6827;
www.house.gov/house/tour_services.shtml

5 Directly across 1st Street is an elaborate memorial to General Ulysses S. Grant.

Ulysses S. Grant (1822–85) achieved international fame as the most important Union military leader during the US Civil War (1861–65). Key battles led by the cool-headed general turned the tide of war in the Union's favour. Moreover, it was Grant who accepted the surrender of Confederate military leader Robert E. Lee that ended the war. Grant served as US president through two terms plagued by scandal and corruption. After leaving the White House, he went bankrupt because of poor business investments. So as not to leave his

WHERE TO EAT

🍽 BULLFEATHERS,
410 First Street, SE;
Tel: 1-202-543-5005.
Watering hole for the House of Representatives since 1980. Casual atmosphere and food. $$

🍽 THE MONOCLE,
107 D Street, NE;
Tel: 1-202-546-4488.
Where members of the Senate go to devour crab cakes and other American fare. Moderately priced bar menu. $$$

family financially destitute, and despite intense pain from terminal cancer, Grant completed his memoirs, finishing the book three days before his death. This memorial was completed in phases between 1909 and 1916.

6 Continue to follow 1st Street along the periphery of the Capitol grounds and then to the intersection of 1st Street and Constitution Avenue, NW. Near the corner is the Robert A. Taft Garden Park.

Senator Robert A. Taft (1889–1953) was the eldest son of 27th US president William Howard Taft. By the 1950s, his hard work and reputation for personal integrity had won him the title 'Mr Republican', although most voters apparently considered him too conservative, too regional, and perhaps

61

a bit too dull to be president: he campaigned for the office three times to no avail. In 1957, after Taft's death, a committee led by Senator John F. Kennedy selected him as one of five of their greatest Senate predecessors whose oval portraits should adorn the President's Room off the Senate floor. This memorial was erected in 1959.

7 From Consitution Avenue, turn right and continue across New Jersey Avenue, NW. Cross Delaware Avenue, NE to the Russell Senate Office Building.

In 1972, this building was named after former Senator Richard Brevard Russell. The Russell Caucus Room inside was used for hearings on the sinking of the Titanic in 1912, the Watergate scandal in 1974, and the nomination of US Supreme Court Justice Clarence Thomas in 1991. Russell represented Georgia from 1933 until his death in 1971. At the time, he was the most senior member of the Senate. Although a highly respected colleague and skilled legislator, Russell disagreed with many of his fellow senators regarding civil rights for African-Americans. In fact, Russell repeatedly blocked and defeated civil-rights legislation. As a result, when Russell made a run at the 1952 Democratic presidential nomination, he was shut out of serious consideration by northern Democrats. Nonetheless, Russell proved a valuable mentor to Texas Senator Lyndon B. Johnson, who was US President between 1963 and 1969 and convinced Congress to pass the Civil Rights Act of 1964.

8 Following Constitution Avenue, cross 1st Street, NE and proceed to 2nd Street, NE. On the corner is the Sewall-Belmont House and Museum.

Mrs Alva Belmont acquired this house in 1929. After a divorce and then the death of her second husband, the wealthy widow devoted her money and leadership to the cause of women's rights. She helped found the National Woman's Party in 1913 and that same year organized a huge suffragette rally in Washington, campaigning to gain women the right to vote. During the march the day before Woodrow Wilson's inauguration in March 1913, unruly behaviour among opponents of women's rights required police intervention to keep order. But the march built momentum for the women's suffrage movement, which succeeded in 1920 with ratification of the 19th Amendment to the Constitution.

SEWALL-BELMONT HOUSE AND MUSEUM;
SAT 11–5, TUE–FRI BY APPOINTMENT;
www.sewallbelmont.org

9 Cross Constitution Avenue and bear right onto Maryland Avenue, NE. At the intersection of 1st Street, turn left. Immediately on the left will be the US Supreme Court.

After the Capitol was set fire to by the British during the War of 1812, a large brick building was quickly erected on this site and Congress met there between 1815 and 1819. The Supreme Court, the highest judicial body in the US, was not constructed here until 1935. Over the entrance to the building is a pediment, which contains the sculpture *Liberty Enthroned Guarded by Order and Authority* by Robert Aitken (1878–1949). Nine figures are featured in the sculpture. Liberty, with the scales of justice in her lap, sits in the centre and is flanked by Roman soldiers, who represent Order and Authority. Beyond them are two pairs of historical figures symbolizing Council – on the left are the building's architect Cass Gilbert (1859–1934) and Elihu Root, a noted lawyer; to the right are Charles Evans Hughes (chief justice 1930–41) and the work's sculptor, Robert Aitken (1878–1949). At the far ends, two more figures represent Research: William Howard Taft (27th US president and chief justice 1921–30) and John Marshall (chief justice 1801–35).

SUPREME COURT OF THE UNITED STATES;

MON–FRI, 9–4.30; www.supremecourtus.gov

10 Stay on 1st Street and cross East Capitol Street. Immediately on the left is the Library of Congress Jefferson Building.

In 1800, Congress voted to purchase books and create a library for its use. From 1800 to 1814, the Library of Congress was housed in various spaces in the Capitol until it was burned. Congress then purchased Thomas Jefferson's personal library to replace their losses. In 1897, this freestanding Library of Congress building opened to the public.

It is known as the Jefferson Building, and with two additional structures named after Presidents John Adams and James Madison it comprises the largest library in the world. It welcomes visiting scholars, the general public and, of course, Congress. The interiors of the Jefferson Building are as ornate as their exterior would suggest. The octagonal main reading room, where 'the opening of a book becomes a noble rite', to quote architectural historian Martin Moeller, is topped by a dome 160ft (48m) high.

LIBRARY OF CONGRESS JEFFERSON BUILDING;

MON–SAT, 10–5; www.loc.gov

11 To get back to Capitol South Metro, follow 1st Street to Independence Avenue, SE. Cross Independence Avenue and continue to D Street, SE. The station will be on the right.

ABOVE: THE ORNATE INTERIOR OF THE LIBRARY OF CONGRESS JEFFERSON BUILDING

STATUES OF PROMINENT AMERICANS IN THE NATIONAL STATUARY HALL IN THE US CAPITOL

Washington during the Civil War

Everywhere you look in central Washington, the story of the US Civil War (1861–65), so crucial to the history of the city, is waiting to be told.

For the first time, what had been a provincial, unimproved capital became the seat of genuine national power. When the war began in May 1861, Washington citizens were catapulted into a world of action and violence, crowds of strangers and an atmosphere of political and military crises. President Abraham Lincoln (1809–65) created the Army of the Potomac to defend the federal capital and thousands of soldiers came to the area. Along Washington's 7th Street corridor, the places where their lives intersected with the war still stand. Greater 7th Street (or Penn Quarter, as it has come to be known) is one of the few parts of central Washington to have retained its 19th-century character. It is full of activity day and night, just as it would have been between 1861 and 1865, though the wartime hospitals, public markets, stables and boarding houses have since evolved into condominiums, restaurants and theatres. Even so, if you set out on a quiet weekend morning, you'll sense the Civil War spirits close at hand.

As you exit the Archives-Navy Memorial-Penn Quarter Metro station, you will see the Prayer of Columbus carved in the granite wall at the foot of the escalator. Poet Walt Whitman (1819–92), its author, was a civilian volunteer during the US Civil War and spent much time in the area you are about to walk through. Outside the station, look for the equestrian statue of General Winfield Scott Hancock directly behind the station exit.

Known to his Army colleagues as 'Hancock the Superb', General Winfield Scott Hancock (1824–86) became a Civil War hero when he led the Union forces to defeat the Confederate army at the Battle of Gettysburg in 1863. During the charge he was shot from his horse, but he continued to command his troops. General Hancock's dress is typical of a US army officer of the time, in particular the broad-brimmed felt hat worn by Union generals. Such was the admiration of Hancock, and so fervent the desire to commemorate US Civil War leaders, that when this statue was unveiled in 1896 every major official in Washington attended.

2 Cross 7th Street, NW at Pennsylvania Avenue, NW. To the left is the memorial dedicated to the Grand Army of the Republic.

The Grand Army of the Republic was a society founded by Dr Benjamin F. Stephenson in 1866. Stephenson conceived the idea of a national society composed of honourably discharged Union soldiers and sailors who were dedicated to assisting disabled soldiers and widows of fallen Union servicemen. Grand Army posts existed in every US state. In fact, the organization wielded such political clout that between 1868 and 1908, no Republican was nominated to the presidency without a Grand Army endorsement. It also played a key part in establishing Decoration Day, which evolved into today's Memorial Day holiday. The Grand Army reached its largest enrolment in 1890, with 490,000 members. In 1956, after the death of the last member, Albert Woolson, the brotherhood was formally dissolved. Its records are archived at the Library of Congress; its badges, flags and official seal at the Smithsonian Institution.

3 Across from the Grand Army of the Republic memorial is a tall building with two conical towers: the headquarters of the National Council of Negro Women.

Founded in 1935, the National Council of Negro Women is a consortium of women's organizations that advocates for women of African descent as they support their families and communities. Built as a hotel during the US Civil War, this entire structure was renovated in the 1980s by combining the hotel with the adjacent commercial structures facing Pennsylvania Avenue. Civil War photographer Mathew Brady (1822–96) had a studio on the upper floor of one of the buildings from 1858 until at

67

DISTANCE **0.5 mile (0.8km)**

ALLOW **I hour (more with site visits)**

START **Archives-Navy Memorial-Penn Quarter Metro station**

FINISH **Metro Center station**

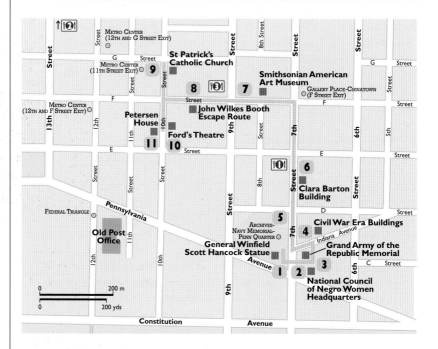

least 1869. One of the most famous photographers of the 19th century, Brady is frequently described as the 'father of photojournalism'. His Civil War portraits and battlefield images conveyed the horror of the conflict to the American public. In the early days, Brady took his photo studio right onto the battlefields. However, he later employed over 20 other photographers, each of whom was given a travelling darkroom, while he stayed in Washington organizing the operation, perhaps due

in part to his deteriorating eyesight. Abraham Lincoln was one of his subjects; his Lincoln photographs have been used for the $5 bill and the Lincoln penny. Although Brady died in New York City, his body was taken to Washington, where he was buried at Congressional Cemetery in the district of Capitol Hill.

4 Walk back towards the Grand Army of the Republic memorial and then proceed to Indiana Avenue, NW. Look at Nos. 637 to 641.

Many of the 19th-century commercial and residential buildings in the city centre were constructed during the boom in development that followed the US Civil War. However, these three structures, dating from 1817 to 1825, represent the streetscape that the thousands of Civil War soldiers marching in and out of Washington would have known.

5 Return to 7th Street and turn right, climbing a small hill. Look for No. 437 on the right.

In 1997, a government employee named Richard Lyons made a remarkable discovery in a sealed crawl space over the third floor of this building: US Civil War artefacts and documents that had been undisturbed for more than 100 years. They identified this structure as the office and residence of Clara Barton (1821–1912), a revered Civil War nurse. When the war broke out, Barton left her position at the US Patent Office and began organizing battlefield relief efforts, bringing supplies to army doctors and nurses. After the war, she located about 22,000 of the 62,000 missing soldiers. She went on to found the American Red Cross in 1881.

6 Continue along 7th Street to the intersection of F Street, NW. Turn left onto F Street at the Smithsonian American Art Museum.

This Smithsonian Museum was originally constructed to house the US Patent Office. Like nearly every other government building in the city, the Patent Office was used for the US Civil War effort. The First Rhode Island Regiment used it as barracks in 1861. Later, it was filled with 2,000 hospital beds for Union soldiers. The famous US poet Walt Whitman was one of the attendants nursing the wounded. The building took on a more festive mood in 1865 as the site for President Lincoln's Second Inaugural Ball. You can walk through the spaces used for this event when visiting the museum and can also find photographs taken by the Mathew Brady Studio as well as portraits of many Civil War-era Americans, including President and Mrs Abraham Lincoln.

SMITHSONIAN AMERICAN ART MUSEUM;

DAILY 11.30–7; www.americanart.si.edu

ABOVE: ENTRANCE TO THE HOME AND OFFICE OF CIVIL WAR NURSE CLARA BARTON

WHERE TO EAT

🍽 CAFÉ ATLANTICO,
405 8th Street, NW;
Tel: 1-202-393-0812.
Mexican, Latin American and
Spanish cuisines come together in
a converted fire station. $$

🍽 SUSHI AOI,
1100 New York Avenue, NW;
Tel: 1-202-408-7770.
Freshly made sushi and udon noodle
soups presented in a Tokyo tech-pop
dining room. $$

🍽 ELLA'S PIZZA,
901 F Street, NW;
Tel: 1-202-638-3434.
Brick-oven baked pizza served in a
convivial atmosphere. $$

7 Looking at the Smithsonian
American Art Museum, turn left
and continue on F Street. Cross 9th
Street, NW, passing especially fine
examples of post-Civil War architecture.
Midway on the left side of the street is
an alleyway.

If you walk to the end of this alley and
look to the right, you view the back of
Ford's Theatre. On 14 April 1865, after
shooting President Abraham Lincoln in
the back of the skull, John Wilkes Booth
fled the theatre. He had injured his left
leg jumping from the presidential box
to the stage. After limping to the horse
he had waiting behind the building,

Booth made his way along this alley to
F Street. Although he managed to escape
to Virginia, federal soldiers eventually
surrounded the tobacco shed in which
he was hiding. When it appeared that
he would shoot his way out, the soldiers
opened fire. Booth died shortly thereafter.

8 Follow F Street to 10th Street,
NW. Turn right and proceed one
block. On the right is St Patrick's
Catholic Church.

The city's first Catholic church is also the
first house of worship of any denomination
founded in Washington. St Patrick's has
been on this site since 1794, but the
cornerstone for the current building was
laid in 1872. Mary Surratt, whose son,
John, was intimately involved with John
Wilkes Booth in the plot to assassinate
Abraham Lincoln, was arrested and put
in prison two days after the president's
death. She operated a boarding house on
H Street, NW, where the men had met
to plot the attack. Mary Surratt, along
with three conspirators, was convicted
and sentenced to death by hanging.
Following her arrest, Mrs Surratt turned
to St Patrick's priest, Father Jacob A.
Walter, for comfort. A staunch defender
of her innocence, Father Walter walked
Surratt to the gallows on 7 July 1865, the
day of her execution. Meanwhile, her
son escaped to Canada and then went
on to England and continental Europe.
He was eventually arrested while living
in Italy and sent back to the US, where
he was put on trial but was later released
following a mistrial in 1868.

9 Return to the F Street intersection, cross the road and continue along 10th Street. On the right is Ford's Theatre.

On 23 May 1865, rows of Union soldiers 60 abreast marched down Pennsylvania Avenue past the US president and General Ulysses S. Grant. So great were their numbers that the procession lasted six hours. They had descended upon America's capital to mark the conclusion of the US Civil War. A mournful air hung over the proceedings, however, because less than one week after Confederate General Robert E. Lee had surrendered, the country was stunned by the news that President Abraham Lincoln had been shot while attending a performance at Ford's Theatre on 14 April. Entrepreneur John T. Ford had recently reopened the venue, following a devastating fire. Now he faced a public demanding the closure of Ford's out of respect for the slain president. After receiving numerous communiqués threatening the destruction of the building and bodily harm to the owner, Ford complied. For almost 90 years, Ford's Theatre offered no live performances, instead serving intermittently as a museum, office space and a storage facility. Following a complete restoration, it reopened in 1968 as a venue for live theatre and a national historic site.

FORD'S THEATRE;

www.fordstheatre.org

10 Across the street from Ford's Theatre is Petersen House at 516 10th Street.

Doctors attending the theatre on 14 April immediately rushed to the wounded Abraham Lincoln. They ordered that the president be brought to the nearest bed, which turned out to be inside a back bedroom of this boarding house. It was here, after a sorrowful vigil, that Lincoln died on the morning of 15 April. He joined 620,000 Union and Confederate soldiers who had also died as a result of the Civil War, the deadliest in US history. Washington was about to embark on a period of unprecedented development, transforming from a muddy backwater town to the grand capital originally envisioned by the nation's first president, George Washington (1732–99). The full restoration of the Union, however, was the work of a contentious post-war era known as Reconstruction. The Reconstruction era lasted from 1866 to 1877 and describes the efforts by the federal government to integrate the southern states back into the Union following the Civil War. A key issue was how those states would develop the means of generating revenue and commercial viability after the dissolution of slavery, upon which much of the Southern economy had been based.

11 To get to Metro Center station, exit Petersen House, turn left and walk half a block to F Street, NW. Turn left on F Street and proceed through the intersections of 11th and 12th Streets, NW. The entrance to the station will be on the left at the corner of 12th and F Streets.

The Tragic Death of a Revered President

The streets of downtown Washington lead to the stately residence where an American president once lived and to the boarding house where he died.

As a young man, Abraham Lincoln (1809–65) 'feared of achieving nothing that would make men remember him'. A single gunshot fired ensured that he would never be forgotten. He served as president during the American Civil War (1861–65), the bloodiest conflict – fought between the North and the South – to have occurred on American soil. Washington was the mould in which Lincoln's momentous years in office were cast. Although the area adjacent to the White House has retained little of its Civil War-era character, if you know where to look, the events of Lincoln's time in the city come to life, whether you are studying a 20th-century office building or a Victorian terrace. The busy streets are much as they would have been in the 1860s, when the president himself made his way, except 21st-century Washingtonians benefit from pavements and Tarmac-covered roads, while in Lincoln's day it would have been a muddy slog. However you make your way, the climax of Lincoln's Washington story – that of the first US leader to be assassinated – was tragic.

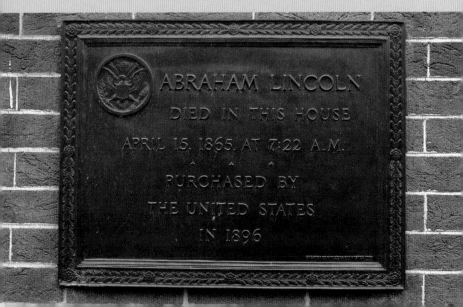

From McPherson Square Metro station at the corner of I Street and Vermont Avenue, NW, cross I Street and then turn right, crossing 15th Street, NW onto McPherson Square.

As commander-in-chief of the US armed forces, President Abraham Lincoln bore ultimate responsibility for the conduct of the Civil War. At the war's outset in 1861, he had witnessed many army and navy officers resign their commission to serve the new 'country' called the Confederate States of America or the Confederacy, which was composed of breakaway southern states. Not so with Major General James Birdseye McPherson, who remained loyal to the president and commanded the Union's Army of the Tennessee. On 22 July 1864, while riding close to Confederate lines during the battle of Atlanta, Georgia, he was shot and killed. This memorial, in McPherson's honour, was unveiled in October 1876.

Cross back onto Vermont Avenue, walking past the Veterans' Administration Building. Look for a bronze plaque on the façade.

Those who work in this building are responsible for administering benefits for veterans, their families and survivors. The Veterans' Administration draws its mission statement from President Lincoln's second inaugural address, in which he wrestled with the moral and religious implications of the Civil War. In the speech's final paragraph, Lincoln delivered his prescription for the nation's recovery:

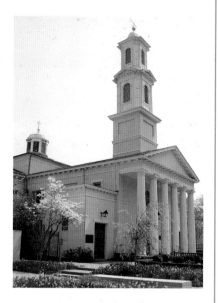

'With malice toward none, with charity for all…let us strive on to finish the work we are in, to bind up the nation's wounds, to care for him who shall have borne the battle and for his widow, and his orphan.'

Follow Vermont Avenue to the end of the block then turn right onto H Street, NW. At the intersection of H and 16th Streets, NW turn right and stand in front of the yellow Episcopal church on the corner.

Lincoln's secretary of state William H. Seward was a member of St John's Church, Lafayette Square. The president himself attended Sunday worship here at least once, but it was on weekdays that he would occasionally slip into a back pew on the south side of the sanctuary during evensong. He would wait until the service had begun and leave before it

73

DISTANCE 1 mile (1.6km)

ALLOW 1 hour (more with museum visits)

START McPherson Square Metro station (White House exit)

FINISH Metro Center station

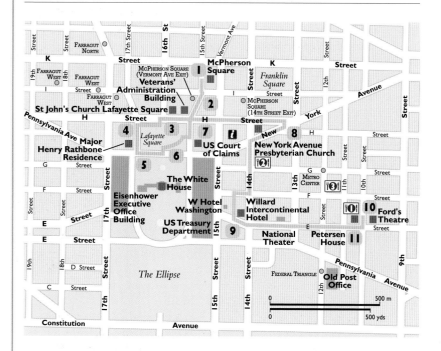

concluded so as not to draw attention to himself, such was his yearning for a few private moments of quiet contemplation.

4 Cross H Street into Lafayette Square, the park on the other side. Turn right and follow H Street to where it intersects with Jackson Place, NW. Turn left and walk along the 19th-century terrace until you come to No. 712.

The night Abraham Lincoln was assassinated proved dire for more than one of his Lafayette Square neighbours. Major Henry Rathbone lived at this house during the Lincoln presidency. It was Rathbone and his fiancée, Clara Harris, who had been invited to attend the theatre with the Lincolns on 14 April 1865, and witnessed the shooting of the president by John Wilkes Booth. Major Rathbone attempted to apprehend the assassin, but Booth stabbed him in the arm, causing Rathbone to let go. Booth fled the theatre and escaped. Rathbone never forgave himself and suffered great mental anguish as a result. So complete was his decline that in December 1893, he inexplicably shot and killed Clara and also stabbed himself repeatedly. He spent the remainder of his life institutionalized.

5 Follow Jackson Place to Pennsylvania Avenue, NW. Walk across, bearing left towards the White House.

The largest room in the White House is the splendid East Room, site of receptions, bill signings and concerts. Yet in 1865 it hosted a much more sombre occasion: the funeral of President Abraham Lincoln. It was not the first sorrowful event to take place in that room while the Lincolns resided there. On 20 April 1862, Willie Lincoln died in one of the upstairs bedrooms at age 11, most probably of typhoid fever. Reverend Phineas D. Gurley of New York Avenue Presbyterian Church presided over the little boy's funeral in the East Room. Willie was the second of Abraham Lincoln's four sons to die of illness, and both he and Mrs Lincoln were devastated. These confrontations with death may be the explanation for a dream Lincoln supposedly had three days before his assassination, in which he prefigured his own death. His friend, Ward Hill Lamon, recollected that the president dreamed he was awoken from sleep by wailing in the White House. After leaving his bedroom, he discovered another room containing only an open coffin with a wrapped corpse inside, and weeping soldiers guarding the coffin burst out, 'The president was killed by an assassin'.

WHERE TO EAT

|O| BISTRO D'OC,
518 10th Street, NW;
Tel: 1-202-393-5444.
Family-owned restaurant featuring specialities from the Languedoc in France and other bistro fare. $$

|O| CEIBA,
701 14th Street, NW;
Tel: 1-202-393-3983.
Contemporary Latin American cuisine served in a colourful dining room inspired by the Yucatan. $$

|O| TOSCA,
1112 F Street, NW;
Tel: 1-202-367-1990.
Italian fine-dining with a hallmark of understated elegance. $$$

6 Cross Pennsylvania Avenue into Lafayette Square. Bear to the right, following the path towards the row of buildings on Madison Place, NW. Proceed to the entrance of the US Court of Claims, the large red-brick structure in the middle of the block.

Lincoln's near-neighbour on Lafayette Square was his secretary of state, William Seward, who resided in a large house that once stood on this site. Like Henry Rathbone, Seward had a traumatic night on 14 April 1865. An assassin working in league with John Wilkes Booth, named Lewis Powell, entered the Seward home with the intent of murdering him.

Booth and his cadre of Confederate sympathizers believed that the chaos of multiple murders committed on one night would throw the Union government into disarray, particularly if those killed included the highest-ranking government officials. Despite being stabbed in the attack, Seward survived and recovered from his wounds. He continued to function as secretary of state in the administration of Lincoln's vice president, Andrew Johnson.

7 Looking at the Court of Claims site, turn left and walk to the end of Madison Place. At the intersection of H Street, turn right. Cross 15th Street, NW. Soon after crossing 14th Street, look for New York Avenue Presbyterian Church on the right. The church is at the intersection of H Street and New York Avenue, NW.

In early 1861, President and Mrs Lincoln began to attend the New York Avenue Presbyterian Church and did so frequently throughout the Civil War. The church has preserved its Lincoln legacy by retaining the president's black hitching post that stands outside the stairs leading to the entrance. The family pew used by the Lincolns has been kept in its original condition in the sanctuary, and a stained-glass window depicts the president at prayer.

8 From there, turn right onto New York Avenue. Follow it one block to 14th Street and turn left onto 14th Street. Continue through G Street, NW

and then to F Street, NW. Cross F Street and turn right. The first entrance on the left is to the Willard Intercontinental Hotel. To the right, off the lobby, is the Willard's 'Hall of History'.

This passageway conveys the unique niche in Washington history occupied by the Willard Hotel. Threat of assassination compelled Detective Daniel A. Pinkerton to smuggle President-elect Abraham Lincoln into the Willard at dawn on 23 February 1861. He and his family stayed until his inauguration 10 days later, returning to the hotel to watch the inaugural parade. Lincoln paid his bill upon receiving his first pay cheque as president – it came to $773.75.

9 Walk through the hotel's Peacock Alley to the main lobby and then exit through the main entrance onto Pennsylvania Avenue. Turn left and cross 14th Street to E Street, NW. Continue along E Street, past the National Theater, and on to 10th Street, NW. Cross 10th Street and turn left. The second building on the right is Ford's Theatre.

President Lincoln and the First Lady arrived at Ford's Theatre on 14 April 1865, after the play *Our American Cousin* had already begun. The couple was led to the presidential box, where Lincoln was seated in a rocking chair on the left-hand side. At about 9pm, John Wilkes Booth arrived at the theatre's back door, armed with a single-shot derringer and a hunting knife. Booth had actually appeared at Ford's Theatre

as an actor and knew his way around. He entered a narrow hallway between the Lincolns' box and the theatre's balcony, barricading the door. Booth was also familiar with the play and waited for the right moment: actor Harry Hawk would be on stage alone and laughter would muffle the sound of a gunshot. At approximately 10.15pm, Booth opened the door to the box and shot Lincoln in the back of the head at near point-blank range.

FORD'S THEATRE;

www.fordstheatre.org

10 Across 10th Street from Ford's Theatre is the Petersen House at No. 516.

Dr Charles Leale, a young Army surgeon, was attending Ford's Theatre on the night of Lincoln's assassination, and became the first doctor to reach Lincoln after the shooting. He and other physicians on hand quickly ascertained that the wound was mortal and ordered the president be removed from Ford's Theatre to the nearest bed. Lincoln was then taken across the street to this boarding house owned by William Petersen. Lincoln's oldest son Robert arrived, followed by secretary of the navy, Gideon Welles, and secretary of war, Edwin Stanton. While Mary Lincoln wept in the front parlour, Stanton took over the running of the US government from a small room adjacent to where Lincoln lay dying. Nothing could be done for the president, and he died on 15 April at 7.22am.

11 To get to Metro Center station, exit the Petersen House, turn left and walk half a block to F Street, NW. Turn left on F Street and proceed through the intersections of 11th and 12th Streets, NW. The station entrance will be on the left, at the corner of 12th and F Streets.

Urban Scavenger Hunt in Penn Quarter

Penn Quarter, bordered to the south by Pennsylvania Avenue, is a vibrant area of the city centre where the 19th century meets the 21st.

Hip hotels, restaurants, luxury condominiums and some of Washington's newest tourist attractions have sprouted up in the area of central Washington recently christened Penn Quarter by developers. That most of these are housed in buildings constructed during the 1800s is what makes this walk an urban scavenger hunt to discover a bygone era – a time when Chinese, German and Italian immigrants lived and worked on and around 7th Street. Unlike other districts in Washington's city centre, Penn Quarter's historic legacy is evident almost everywhere you look, creating an outdoor museum of 19th-century residential, religious and government buildings. These provide the backdrop for a street scene bustling with residents, theatre- and cinema-goers, bar hoppers, and shoppers – especially at night. Yet what makes a walk through Penn Quarter particularly rewarding is discovering the stories behind the buildings – of the people who inhabited them a century ago. Follow this walk route to meet them.

Exiting Archives-Navy Memorial-Penn Quarter Metro station, turn right and then immediately right again, walking past a restaurant and bank to 7th Street, NW. Cross the street and continue along Indiana Avenue, NW to No. 641, the Artifactory Building.

Importer Dominick Cardella has used this 1817 commercial building for both work and home since 1972. He is the last businessman in Penn Quarter to live as the 19th-century immigrants once did, with their shops on the ground floor and their living accommodation above the shop. Cardella's emporium for African and Asian artefacts takes up the ground floor, he rents the first floor to an attorney, and lives in a spacious, light-filled loft on the second floor. If the shop is open, do stop in and say hello. Also, peek into No. 637 two doors away. It was formerly Litwin's Furniture, operated by the same family since the 1920s, when family-run furniture stores proliferated in the area. Although a national sandwich chain has taken over, the vintage Otis elevator has been preserved.

2 Double back to 7th Street and turn right. Continue to the intersection of F Street, NW, turn left, and proceed to the Hotel Monaco on the left.

This building, designed by architect Robert Mills (1781–1855), who also designed the Washington Monument, served as the city's General Post Office between 1842 and 1897. German immigrants who started arriving in the city from the 1850s on might have sought a job in one of those offices; for people who had held positions as clerks, accountants or even messengers back home, a major government agency like the post office offered good potential employment. In 2000, the then-vacant building underwent a stunning restoration to turn it into a luxury hotel.

3 Across F Street from the Hotel Monaco is the Smithsonian Museum of American Art and National Portrait Gallery.

Construction for this structure, designed by Robert Mills and originally the US Patent Office, began in 1836. In addition to its employees, the building drew more than 100,000 visitors annually as the de facto national museum, before the Smithsonian Castle was completed in 1855. Boyd's *Washington City Directory* wrote, 'You may see the models of most

DISTANCE I mile (1.6km)

ALLOW 1.5 hours (more with museum visits)

START Archives-Navy Memorial-Penn Quarter Metro station

FINISH Judiciary Square Metro station (F Street exit)

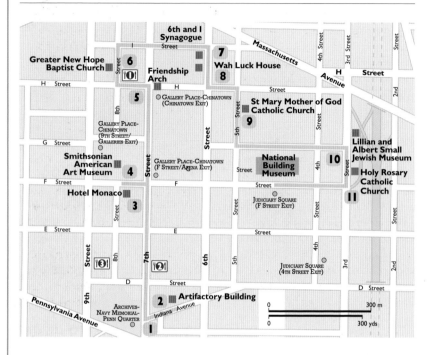

everything that has ever been invented or grown out of the Yankee brain'. For a young German immigrant renting a room on 6th Street, NW, the Patent Office provided inspiration. Emile Berliner, with no background in science but blessed with a patient landlady who allowed him to string wires between the house and the barn out at the back, invented a microphone that captured the human voice via magnetic current: it revolutionized telephone technology. Berliner later developed a means of

recording sound vibrations on the sides of a groove spiralled onto a flat disk: this evolved into the long-playing record. He filed patents for these as well as his other inventions at this building.

SMITHSONIAN AMERICAN ART MUSEUM;

DAILY 11.30–7; www.americanart.si.edu

4 Double back to 7th Street and turn left. After you cross G Street, NW, notice the Chinese characters on the shop fronts, signalling that you have

entered the Chinatown district. The name of the bank on the corner of 7th and G Streets is Oriental Business Association (OBA). Surprisingly, it was founded by German rather than Chinese immigrants. The pediments of Nos. 714 and 718 7th Street still bear the names of the original immigrant business owners and residents. Proceed to the intersection of 7th and H Streets, NW.

The world's largest single-span Chinese arch designates the heart of what was once a small but thriving Chinatown. Chinese immigrants first arrived in Washington in the 1880s, having journeyed from the western states, where work had become scarce and discrimination common. They initially settled along Pennsylvania Avenue, not far from the US Capitol, but in 1931 the community was forced to relocate to the H Street area to make way for the construction of a municipal centre. Later, in the mid 1980s, part of the new Chinatown was again displaced to enable the construction of the Washington Convention Center. Although most Chinese-American families have since moved out of the city centre to live in the suburbs, their restaurants and shops have remained in this district. A current form of economic prosperity for the Chinese-Americans is the express bus service that they operate between Washington and New York City.

5 Turn left onto H Street and continue to 8th Street, NW. Turn right on 8th Street and proceed to the imposing Greater New Hope Baptist Church.

In the mid-19th century, Washington's Jewish population was largely of German origin. The first Jewish congregation formed as Washington Hebrew in 1852. Eleven years later, the members purchased a church located on this site, altering its appearance to reflect the Jewish faith. By 1897, Washington Hebrew was able to replace that building with the one you see today (although it is missing the original onion domes that topped the towers). The synagogue was the largest in the city and a vital resource for the many Jews who lived in the area. When many of its members opted for life in the suburbs, Washington Hebrew built a new synagogue in northwest Washington, selling its former home to Greater New Hope Baptist Church in 1954.

6 Looking at the church, turn right and proceed to I Street, NW. Turn right again and follow it across 7th Street, to the intersection of 6th and I Streets, NW.

By the early 1860s, Washington Hebrew Congregation began to introduce reform practices into the services, allowing women to sit with men and using English or German for the sermon and some prayers. When the congregation bought an organ in 1869, 38 members resigned to form a more traditional Orthodox congregation called Adas Israel. In 1908, having outgrown their small wooden synagogue, Adas Israel moved into the gracious domed building on the corner. Like Washington Hebrew, Adas Israel's members also relocated to the suburbs in the 1940s and 1950s, inspiring

WHERE TO EAT

[O] MATCHBOX,
713 H Street, NW;
Tel: 1-202-289-4441.
The brick oven is always busy baking
New York-style pizza. $$

[O] OYAMEL COCINA MEXICANA,
401 7th Street, NW;
Tel: 1-202-628-1005.
Chef José Andrés creates innovative
dishes inspired by the urban fare of
Mexico City. $$

[O] TEAISM,
400 8th Street, NW;
Tel: 1-202-638-6010
Simple and delicious Bento boxes
from Japan, curries from Thailand, and
tandoor breads from India. $$

construction of a third worship space
in northwest Washington. In 1952, the
6th and I Historic Synagogue became
the Turner Memorial African-American
Episcopal Church. The church remained
here for nearly 50 years before putting
the building on the market in 2001.
The estate agent's brochure described
the structure as 'suitable for a nightclub'.
Alarmed that such an important reminder
of the city's Jewish odyssey was in peril,
the Jewish Historical Society worked with
three prominent Washington developers
with historic ties to the building to
purchase it for $5 million. The synagogue
was restored to its 1908 state and now
offers Friday-evening Shabbat services

and Saturday worship, as well as concerts
and lectures, echoing its original use as a
gathering place for Jewish Washington.

7 Turn right and proceed along 6th
Street to the corner of 6th and H
Streets. The large apartment house on
the corner is Wah Luck House.

More than 200 Chinese-American
families, many of them senior citizens,
lost their homes when displaced by
the construction of the Washington
Convention Center on the western edge
of Chinatown in the 1980s. Wah Luck
House was built in 1982, in exchange
for the loss of housing. It is one of the
few residences in the area still occupied
by Chinese-Americans.

8 Cross H Street and turn left,
following H Street one block to 5th
Street, NW. Turn right on 5th Street and
stand in front of St Mary Mother of God
Catholic Church.

This is a remarkable spot in Penn
Quarter: a small campus of religious
structures developed by German
Catholic immigrants soon after arriving
in Washington. The Gothic church was
constructed in 1890. The rectory next
door came next, followed by what used
to be St Mary's Orphanage and St
Mary's School. (The orphanage building
can be seen at the end of the alley
that runs next to the school.) Each is
a testament to the German Catholics'
desire to meet the spiritual and social
needs of its immigrant congregation, as

well as providing a means of maintaining a German identity. Notice the sign advertising worship in Cantonese, a nod to the Chinese-Americans who eventually moved into the parish.

9 Follow 5th Street to G Street and turn left. Proceed along two long blocks to 3rd Street, NW. You will pass the enormous General Accountability Office headquarters on the left and the stately National Building Museum on the right. At the terminus of G Street at 3rd Street you will see the first synagogue constructed in Washington.

When the 38 members of Washington Hebrew left to form their own congregation, they initially prayed in rented spaces while they raised funds to build a synagogue of their own. By 1876, the congregation had raised $4,800 and built their new synagogue in the heart of the Jewish community – at the southeast corner of 6th and G Streets, NW. The synagogue is the oldest in the nation's capital and among the oldest in the country. The most distinctive feature is the original, semi-circular, protruding Aron Kodesh (Holy Ark), the cabinet at the front of a synagogue in which the sacred Torah scrolls are kept. In 1968, the synagogue was slated for demolition when the Washington Metropolitan Area Transit Authority acquired the entire city block for its new headquarters. The Jewish Historical Society mobilized the community, saving the building with assistance from local and federal governments. On 18 December 1969,

the 237-ton synagogue was moved three city blocks to its current site. After it was moved, it reopened as the Lillian and Albert Small Jewish Museum.

LILLIAN AND ALBERT SMALL JEWISH MUSEUM;

OPEN BY APPOINTMENT; www.jhsgw.org

10 Turn right and walk one block along 3rd Street to the small Holy Rosary Catholic Church on the left.

A sizeable number of Italians emigrated to Washington at the turn of the 20th century. Many were skilled masons brought in to build and adorn monumental public buildings, such as the Library of Congress and Union Station. They were frequently shunned by the more established Catholics in the city, prompting the new Italian community to request an Italian-speaking priest. In 1916, this land was purchased and in 1919 work began on Holy Rosary Catholic Church, which from its inception has promoted and preserved Italian Catholic heritage and culture.
In fact, the order of priests serving the church, the Scalabrini Missionaries, has as its purpose the pastoral and social care of migrants from Italy. Italian language classes are offered at Casa Italiana, the parish hall next door to the church.

11 From Holy Rosary, turn right onto F Street. Walk one block and then look for the entrance to the Judiciary Square Metro station. It is located across the street from the National Building Museum.

History and Culture in Foggy Bottom

The Foggy Bottom Historic District, one of Washington's oldest neighbourhoods, is an oasis of calm in the middle of this fast-paced city.

Originally a little port town called Hamburg, Foggy Bottom was later the site of two breweries, a gas works and other light industry. While the district has lost its industrial character, you can still explore Foggy Bottom's alleys and courts and discover the neat rows of houses that blue-collar workers called home. One of the smallest residential areas in the city, Foggy Bottom's historic district is tucked away between the George Washington University campus and the Rock Creek Parkway. It's a place of contrasts between high rises and small terraced houses, peaceful alleyways and relentless traffic. One moment you'll be standing before some of the tiniest houses in Washington, the next you'll be exploring the Watergate complex, one of the city's largest residential developments. The finale to any walk through Foggy Bottom is a visit to the John F. Kennedy Center for the Performing Arts. Time your walk to finish around 6pm, when free daily performances sponsored by the Kennedy Center begin.

1 Step outside Foggy Bottom Metro station and turn right onto 23rd Street, NW, passing a large bust of the George Washington University's namesake. Notice a dorm named after First Lady Jacqueline Kennedy across the street. She earned a BA here. Proceed to St Mary's Church at 728 23rd Street.

Two years after the US Civil War (1861–65), a group of newly emancipated slaves formed an Episcopal congregation, called St Mary's, and began worshipping at the refurbished Union Army Chapel, on the site of the present St Mary's Church. In 1887, assisted financially by the congregations of St John's Lafayette Square and the Church of the Epiphany, St Mary's hired Smithsonian Institution architect James Renwick (1818–95) to design this church. The Foggy Bottom district was the recipient of the church's various ministries through the years, including the organization of one of the first Boys Clubs in the city, a clinic for infants, sewing and cooking schools, and facilities for mentally disabled children. It is the oldest African-American Episcopal congregation in Washington.

2 Continue along 23rd Street to the intersection of G Street, NW. Turn right and then right again on 24th Street, NW. At No. 725 is St Mary's Court.

Parishioners from St Mary's Church urged the Episcopal Diocese of Washington to create affordable housing for senior citizens here in Foggy Bottom. St Mary's Court is the result of those efforts. Over 150 senior citizens reside here in individual apartments. The Episcopal Diocese continues to sponsor the residence, with the Department of Housing and Urban Development providing the funding.

3 Follow 24th Street past St Mary's Court to the intersections of I Street and New Hampshire Avenue, NW. Bear right onto New Hampshire Avenue. Continue until it intersects with Washington Circle. Carefully cross the street onto the circle.

Washington Circle has always been an important crossroads in northern Foggy Bottom, originally connecting the area to Lafayette Park to the east and Georgetown to the west. The vistas down Pennsylvania Avenue and K Street are amazing for around 12 blocks. See for yourself via a promenade around the circle. The equestrian statue of George Washington captures a crucial moment in the American War of Independence: a surprise attack on the British forces at Princeton and Trenton, New Jersey. This was the first memorial to Washington in the city, unveiled in 1860.

4 Exit the circle onto Pennsylvania Avenue. Follow it one block to 24th Street, NW. On the corner across the street is 2401 Pennsylvania Avenue.

Examine the exterior of this building closely. The architectural firm of Keyes Condon Florance added a few whimsical touches to this office building, erected

85

DISTANCE 1 mile (1.6km)

ALLOW 1 hour

START **Foggy Bottom Metro station**

FINISH **Foggy Bottom Metro station**

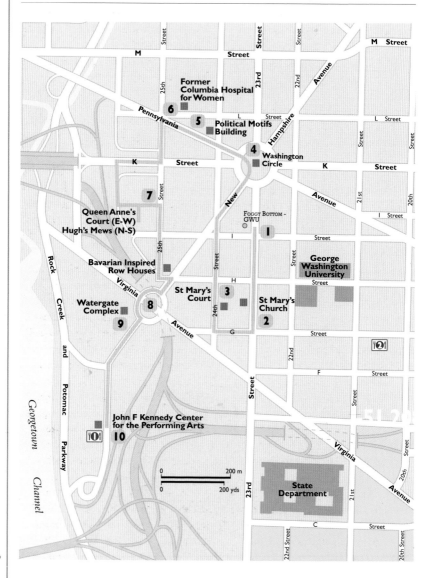

in 1991. What better than political motifs for a building with a Pennsylvania Avenue address? Elephants, symbolizing the Republican Party, and donkeys, for the Democrats, form the brackets holding the cables that support the ground-floor canopies. A stars and stripes 'banner' unfurls along the roofline right into the US and District of Columbia flags.

5 Continue one block to the intersection of 25th Street, NW. Across the street is the Columbia Residences of Washington, DC.

Some of the female homeowners residing in this handsome condominium may have memories of giving birth here when the building housed the Columbia Hospital for Women. The hospital was founded during the US Civil War to assist destitute women, many of whom had arrived in the city seeking information about relatives who were injured or imprisoned. The enormous Ringgold House, built here in 1812, was converted into a hospital in 1872 and was then razed to the ground in 1914, when the structure now occupied by the condominiums was built. Columbia Hospital for Women closed in 2002.

6 Turn left onto 25th Street, NW from Pennsylvania Avenue. Cross K Street and then turn right onto K Street. One block later, turn left onto 26th Street, NW. The first left is Queen Anne's Court. Turn into it and then turn right into Hugh's Mews. At the end of the alley is a group of tiny terraced houses.

WHERE TO EAT

🍽 KC CAFÉ,
John F. Kennedy Center for the Performing Arts,
New Hampshire Avenue, NW and Rock Creek Parkway;
Tel: 1-202-416-8555.
Upmarket cafe on the roof terrace of the Kennedy Center, perfect for a quick bite before a performance. $$

🍽 TONIC RESTAURANT AT QUIGLEY'S PHARMACY,
2036 G Street, NW;
Tel: 1-202-296-0211.
Historic drug store on the George Washington University campus, serving comfort food with a twist. $$

During the first half of the 19th century, Foggy Bottom was a working-class riverfront settlement populated largely by Irish and German immigrants. Two breweries and the Washington Gas Light Company offered employment, and these alley houses provided inexpensive accommodation. Once the area's identity had shifted from industry to a precinct of government headquarters, the original homeowners moved on. Houses like these were then occupied by poorer, disenfranchised residents who could not afford to move. Living conditions in the alleys had deteriorated to such a sorry state that by the 1950s, large swathes of Foggy Bottom were selected for urban renewal. Some, but not all, of the alley houses were selected for preservation.

This explains the juxtaposition of the small-scale alley houses to the looming high rises constructed around them.

7 Exit Hugh's Mews and turn right onto Queen Anne's Court. At the intersection of 25th Street, turn right and proceed along 25th Street.

You are passing through the heart of the small Foggy Bottom Historic District. The Flemish gables, tall, narrow lancet windows and peaked lintels adorning the terraced houses on this block were designed to remind the Germans who emigrated to Foggy Bottom in the 19th century of their homeland architecture.

8 At the end of 25th Street is the massive Watergate complex.

Before it became synonymous with political scandal, the term Watergate was a direct allusion to the water gate at the edge of the Potomac River, due west of the Lincoln Memorial and flanking the Arlington Memorial Bridge. The Water Gate Inn once stood near this site and a floating water-gate barge once hosted concerts. The presidential political scandal received its name from the Watergate office building, where Republican operatives broke into the Democratic National Committee headquarters. This huge development was constructed between 1965 and 1971 and included three apartments, one office and one hotel building placed in a garden setting overlooking the Potomac. Italian architect Luigi Moretti (1907–73) was said to have

been inspired by the beautiful curvilinear terraces in Bath, England. Unfortunately for local residents, the complex blocks what used to be an unobstructed view of the river. You can glimpse the water if you go into the building, towards the back.

9 Looking at the main entrance of the Watergate complex, turn left onto New Hampshire Avenue, NW. You will pass the Saudi Arabian Embassy on the left and then arrive at the stairway leading to the John F. Kennedy Center for the Performing Arts.

Dedicated in 1971, the Kennedy Center is not only the largest performing arts venue in the city, but also the Washington memorial to President John F. Kennedy, who was assassinated in 1963. It's an active place, with performances every day of the year by groups such as the Washington National Opera and National Symphony Orchestra in addition to ballet, theatre and jazz. Each day at 6pm the Millennium Stage presents a wide variety of free programmes. Visit the gift shop, take a tour, and, without question, take the lift up to the roof terrace and step outside. More splendid, panoramic views of the Potomac riverfront cannot be found.

10 An easy way to return to Foggy Bottom Metro station is to catch a free shuttle bus from outside the front entrance of the Kennedy Center. The red minibuses run from morning until the last performance of the day, transporting Kennedy Center guests to and from the station.

OPPOSITE: THE GRAND FOYER OF THE JOHN F. KENNEDY CENTER FOR THE PERFORMING ARTS

THE JOHN F. KENNEDY CENTER, THE LARGEST PERFORMING ARTS VENUE IN THE CITY

Elegant Circles and Squares

Discover Logan Circle, the city's only unaltered Victorian residential district, just a short walk from the heart of downtown Washington.

Few areas of Washington have witnessed the dramatic change and breathtaking renaissance of Logan Circle, which evolved from rural obscurity to an enclave of elegance, home to wealthy white and later African-American residents. If you're a fan of Victorian Gothic Revival architecture, this walk is for you. If you're fascinated by the dynamics of urban neighbourhoods, consider the residents of Logan Circle: their tenacity and vision preserved the historic district when it teetered on the brink of decline. Today, it is one of the most sought-after addresses in Washington. Impressive restoration and renovation continues, and restaurants and shops multiply. This is a fun expedition to set out on in the afternoon. As the hapless commuters climb into their cars to battle traffic, you'll be following the denizens of Logan Circle home on foot, soon to be walking their dogs in the shadow of John Logan's statue. Then it's on to a cafe or bar for a quick drink before dinner. You'll be finishing your walk just in time to join them.

I Leave McPherson Square Metro station, 14th Street exit, and turn right. From the corner of 14th and I Streets, NW cross I Street and then turn right to cross 14th Street into Franklin Square. Standing along the 14th Street side of the park is a statue of Commodore John Barry.

From 1920 on, Irish-Americans decided to mark St Patrick's Day by processing from St Patrick's Roman Catholic Church some blocks away to lay a wreath at the feet of this statue. Barry, a young Irish-American sea captain, became the first American naval officer to capture an enemy ship during the War of American Independence (1775–83). Congress erected this monument at the request of Irish-Americans, who attended the unveiling ceremony in the thousands on 16 May 1914.

2 Walk across the park to the other side, which is bordered by 13th Street, NW. The exuberant Victorian Franklin School will come into view. Look towards the top of the building for a small bust of Benjamin Franklin (1706–90), the US statesman, scientist and inventor after whom the school (and the square) was named.

Completed in 1869, Franklin School was designed by German-born Adolf Cluss (1825–1905), one of Washington's most influential and progressive architects. Cluss's ideas on how to build modern, multi-roomed state schools with adequate ventilation and space for students and teachers reflect the influence of the socialist circles he had been part of before emigrating to the US. At the time, the Franklin School was considered to be an outstanding Washington state school located in what was then a fashionable residential area. However, when these homeowners moved out of Franklin Square to the area northwest of the city centre, the district began a slow decline, reaching its nadir in the 1970s and 1980s, when prostitution, pornography and the drug trade infested what was left of the glorious 19th-century built environment. Developers took matters into their own hands in 1990, commencing with a transformation of Franklin Square into a precinct of commercial office buildings.

3 Return to 14th Street along K Street, NW. At the intersection of K and 14th Streets, turn right and proceed on 14th Street until it intersects with Thomas Circle. Bear to the left and travel around the circle until you reach the steps of National City Christian Church.

Thomas Circle, named after General George H. Thomas, whose statue stands in its centre, first developed as a quiet area of handsome townhouses framed by the beautiful Victorian gas lamps that illuminated the circle's perimeter. Located at the intersection of what became three major Washington thoroughfares, Thomas Circle was probably destined to be overtaken by the automobile in the 20th century, as the numerous traffic lanes winding around it prove. The National City Christian Church was completed

DISTANCE 1.5 miles (2.5km)

ALLOW 1.5 hours (more with museum visit)

START McPherson Square Metro station (14th Street exit)

FINISH McPherson Square Metro station (14th Street exit)

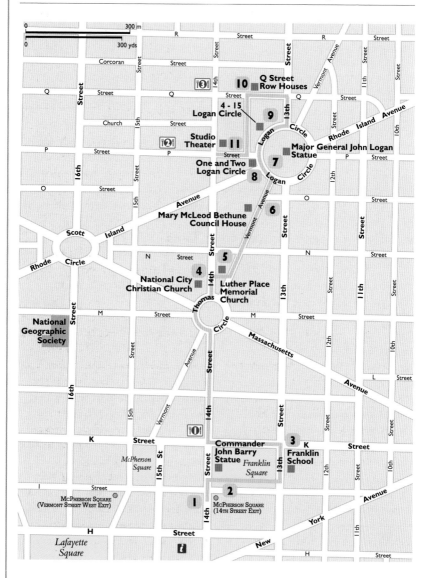

in 1930 by the Disciples of Christ, a Protestant denomination based in North America. The original sanctuary still stands nearby on Vermont Avenue, NW. The limestone edifice cost $1.2 million and was designed by John Russell Pope (1874–1937), architect of the Thomas Jefferson Memorial.

4 Cross 14th Street to Luther Place Memorial Church.

Soon after the US Civil War (1861–65), Lutherans in Washington built this church as a memorial to peace. It is the only remaining evidence of the 19th-century Thomas Circle, its High Victorian Gothic Revival style rendering it particularly impressive. The church did not receive its present name until the unveiling of the statue of Martin Luther (1483–1546), German theologian and leader of the Protestant Reformation, in May 1884. It is a copy of a statue in Worms, Germany, and was erected to commemorate the 400th anniversary of Luther's birth.

5 Facing the statue of Martin Luther, turn right onto Vermont Avenue and begin your walk into the heart of the Logan Circle Historic District. The church on the left, Mount Olivet Lutheran Church, occupies the building first used by the Disciples of Christ for worship. The houses you will pass next were built between 1874 and 1876. Stop in front of No. 1318.

The Mary McLeod Bethune Council House honours one of the most

WHERE TO EAT

🍽 **DC COAST,**
1401 K Street, NW;
Tel: 1-202-216-5988.
Knock-out dining room serving the coastal cuisines of the Mid-Atlantic, Gulf of Mexico and West Coast. $$$

🍽 **LOGAN TAVERN,**
1423 P Street, NW;
Tel: 1-202-332-3710.
Upscale but casual restaurant serving sophisticated comfort food. Don't miss the Bloody Mary menu during weekend brunch. $$

🍽 **RICE,**
1608 14th Street, NW;
Tel: 1-202-234-2400.
Imaginative Thai restaurant, with a Zen-like atmosphere. $$

remarkable African-American leaders of the 20th century. A tireless educator born to former slaves, Mary McLeod Bethune (1875–1955) is best known for founding a school in 1904 that later became part of Bethune-Cookman University in Daytona Beach, Florida. One of the few women in the world to serve as a college president at that time, she was later a member of President Franklin D. Roosevelt's Black Cabinet. In 1935, Bethune founded the National Council of Negro Women, bringing together 28 different organizations to form a council to facilitate the improvement of quality of life for African-American women and

champion their cause. For example, Logan and his wife were instrumental in organizing the first Memorial Day in 1868. A US federal holiday, Memorial Day is observed on the last Monday of May and commemorates US men and women who perished while in military service. The Logans lived at 4 Logan Circle between 1884 and 1885, when this was called Iowa Circle. It was not until 1930 that Congress passed a law changing the name to Logan. The statue was unveiled in 1901. It is unique in Washington in that the elaborate pedestal is made of bronze, not granite. A figure representing Peace is north of the statue; and one representing War on the south. Panels on the east and west sides depict Logan as statesman and general.

children. She bought this house in 1943, making it the first headquarters of that organization, and lived there until 1949. **MARY MCLEOD BETHUNE COUNCIL HOUSE;** MON–SAT 9–5; WWW.NPS.GOV/ MAMC

6 Continue to follow Vermont Avenue until it intersects with Logan Circle. Cross the street to the circle itself, standing in front of the equestrian statue of Major General John Logan.

John A. Logan was a member of the House of Representatives from Illinois when the US Civil War broke out in 1861. He recruited the 31st Illinois Regiment and was promoted to colonel. He became tremendously popular among veterans as someone who would

7 Across from the Logan statue is a large, white, Second Empire style building at Nos. 1 and 2 Logan Circle.

After the US Civil War, impressive homes such as this began to appear on what had been considered barren land. These substantial adjoining townhouses were built in 1878 and are a typical example of the architectural style known as Second Empire, which was popular with wealthy Victorian-era Washingtonians between the 1850s and 1880s. A hipped or mansard roof, porthole windows and a double entranceway are all characteristic of this style. In 1921, the building was converted to apartments and began a slow period of decline. By the 1970s, the entire area was infested with prostitutes and drug addicts. This was the first property to be restored by a developer after years of neglect. The P N Hoffman company purchased it in 1998 and lovingly brought it back to life.

8 From 1 and 2 Logan Circle, cross P Street, NW and look at the houses at numbers 4 to 15 Logan Circle.

Logan Circle has a variety of High Victorian-era residential buildings and is one of only two circles in Washington to have retained its residential character completely. Not all of the houses, however, are original. Can you spot the new construction at 27 to 30 Logan Circle? The row of eclectic homes in front of you, however, is authentic, the façades having changed little since the residences were first constructed. A few remain family homes, though most have been subdivided, a trend that began in the 1940s. From the 1930s, prominent African-Americans began to inhabit many of these homes. No. 8 belonged to Belford V. Lawson and Marjorie M. Lawson, an esteemed lawyer and the first black woman to serve on a local court in Washington. Their neighbour at No. 11 was Charles Manuel 'Sweet Daddy' Grace, founder of the United House of Prayer, an African-American church with millions of members throughout the world.

9 Just after No. 15, bear right onto 13th Street, NW. Proceed one block to Q Street, NW then turn left. Notice the row of brightly coloured houses.

These homes, constructed between 1876 and 1878, are perfect examples of the rows of middle-class speculative houses built throughout Washington in the late 19th and early 20th centuries. They are joined by party walls, and ornamental detail has been placed only on the buildings' facades. Builders often ordered prefabricated materials for these houses from catalogues in order to keep expenses down. This meant that owners of modest means could duplicate, on a smaller scale, the mansions of the well-to-do.

10 Follow Q Street to the intersection of Kingman Place, NW and turn right. The modest homes on this block were built to house lower-income residents who might have worked for the wealthy home owners on the circle. At the intersection of P Street, turn right, stopping at the corner of 14th and P Streets.

The Studio Theater moved to this space in 1987, a pioneer in an area few businesses were willing to consider investing in. This building was formerly occupied by Petrovitch Motors, one of the numerous car dealerships and showrooms that sprang up along 14th Street from the 1920s on. The enormous windows were to provide optimal viewing of the shiny new cars inside.

11 To get back to McPherson Square Metro, turn left and follow 14th Street to Thomas Circle. Bear right, walking halfway around the circle and exiting back onto 14th Street. Cross L and K Streets, NW. The station is at the intersection of 14th and I Streets, NW.

THOMAS CIRCLE, NAMED AFTER GENERAL GEORGE H. THOMAS, WHOSE STATUE IS IN ITS CENTRE

A Feast for the Senses at Kalorama

Kalorama – Greek for 'beautiful view' – certainly lives up to its name, with its natural ambience, elegant mansions and international flavour.

Joel Barlow named the estate he purchased in 1807 Kalorama for the expansive views it enjoyed in its elevated position. The 90 acres (36 hectares) remained intact until 1887, when they were divided into smaller plots. The development that followed retained the hilly character, topography and densely planted trees, with the entire northern boundary of the district overlooking the picturesque Rock Creek Park. Undoubtedly the most beautiful part of Washington, Kalorama has always been a prime residential area, with its urban mansions located on the high ground between Massachusetts and Connecticut Avenues, the enclave seen on this walk. You start by ascending the Spanish Steps to reach the heights where Washington's diplomatic community is evident everywhere you look – many of the residences are occupied by ambassadors or function as embassies. Old phone boxes that once had a direct line to the police or fire brigade punctuate the area and are now considered works of art.

1 Leave Dupont Circle Metro station from the Q Street exit, turn right onto 20th Street, NW and follow it to the intersection of R Street, NW. Turn left onto R Street. At the intersection of 22nd Street, NW turn right. Proceed for one block and you will arrive at the Decatur Terrace Steps (also known as the Spanish Steps), at the intersection of 22nd Street and Decatur Place, NW.

Notice the two police and fire-brigade phone boxes on the corner. These were installed throughout Washington from the 1860s on, before the advent of the 911 emergency services. Too large and heavy to be removed after they became obsolete, the phone boxes have been 'reinvented' by Cultural Tourism DC as works of art. You'll find several on this route. Across the road from the phone boxes is 2145 Decatur Place. Today, the Thai ambassador resides in this house. Notice how the garden terrace and house itself act as a massive retaining wall for the Decatur Terrace slope. Martha Codman was the original owner, her cousin Ogden Codman, Jr having designed the house for her in 1907. Both would have been society celebrities to their Kalorama neighbours: Martha contributed to Edith Wharton's classic book *Decoration of Houses*, which Wharton co-wrote with Ogden. Moreover, Ogden was the architect of choice for the wealthy Vanderbilts and Rockefellers of New York.

2 Climb the Decatur Terrace Steps to S Street, NW. At the top of the steps on the right is 1743 22nd Street, NW.

A noted palaeontologist, Charles D. Wolcott became secretary of the Smithsonian Institution in 1907, just two years after completing this Italianate mansion. The cheerful panda sculpture greeting visitors was one of dozens on display throughout Washington during a public art exhibition called Pandamania.

3 Turn right onto S Street and then left onto Phelps Place, NW. At the intersection of California Street, NW is Our Lady, Queen of the Americas Roman Catholic Church on the left.

The entrance to the church is at 2200 California Street. At 1836 Phelps Place is the entrance to what was St Rose's Industrial School, founded in 1872 to educate orphan girls in home economics and other domestic arts. It is one of the few buildings in Kalorama that was not built as a residence.

4 Turn left on California Street then right onto 23rd Street, NW. On the corner of 23rd and Wyoming Streets, NW is 2300 Wyoming Street.

Anthony Francis Lucas was the original owner of this mansion. A mechanical engineer who had emigrated from Croatia, Lucas was responsible for the first successful oil well at Spindletop oil field in southeast Texas, turning unassuming Beaumont into one of the first oil boomtowns. On 10 January 1901, a gas eruption occurred, followed by a stream of crude oil spewing up nearly 200ft (60m). The eruption lasted nine days.

DISTANCE **1 mile (1.6km)**

ALLOW **1 hour (more with museum visit)**

START **Dupont Circle Metro station (Q Street exit)**

FINISH **Dupont Circle Metro station (Q Street exit)**

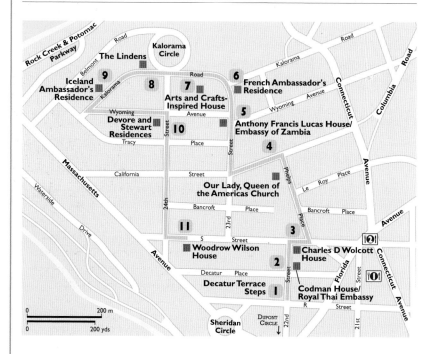

5 Continue along 23rd Street. At the next intersection it becomes Kalorama Road. Soon after the intersection, on the right at No. 2221, is an enormous house that resembles a Tudor country manor.

This is the largest house in Kalorama. It was constructed in 1911 for William Watson Lawrence, a successful businessman from Pittsburgh, Pennsylvania. It was designed by Jules H. de Sibour, architect of many Embassy

Row and Kalorama mansions. When Watson died, he was living in New York City and had no heirs, so he willed all his Washington property to his two unmarried sisters who resided here. The government of France purchased the house in 1936 for about $400,000, including furnishings. It has been the French ambassador's residence ever since.

6 One block further along Kalorama Road and across the street is No. 2340.

Built in 1928, this house was designed not as an Italianate or French mansion, but in the Arts and Crafts style. This design style, which strived to revive medieval craftsmanship, originated in Britain in the late 19th century but was popularized in the early 20th century in the US by architect/designers Gustav Stickley and the two brothers, Charles S. and Henry M. Greene.

7 Across the street at 2401 Kalorama Road is the Lindens.

Dating from 1745, the Lindens is the oldest house in Washington. However, it was not built on this site. Instead, the Georgian house was constructed in Danvers, Massachusetts, where it remained until 1936, when the owners Mr and Mrs George Morris moved it to Washington so that they could house their extensive antique collection. The rebuilding probably saved the house, because prior to the move Lindens was crumbling and in danger of being destroyed. Before it was dismantled, the house was carefully documented with precise drawings and photographs so that it could be erected easily in its new position. The Morrises hired Walter Macomber, resident architect at Colonial Williamsburg, to direct the project, which took 34 months to complete.

8 Continue on Kalorama Road to No. 2443 on the right.

The Icelandic ambassador resides in this charming brick house, which dates from 1927. Interestingly, the Embassy of Iceland in Washington also represents Iceland

ABOVE: THE LINDENS, THE OLDEST HOUSE IN WASHINGTON

in Argentina, Brazil, Chile, El Salvador, Guatemala and Mexico. One wonders how often the ambassador is at home!

9 Follow Kalorama Road until it intersects with Wyoming Street. Turn left and follow Wyoming Street to the end of the block, where it intersects with 24th Street, NW. Stop in front of 2000 24th Street.

Two daughters of Congressman Alexander Stewart, a lumber magnate from Wisconsin, built this house and the one at 2030 24th Street. One sister hired architect William L. Bottomley to design this two-storey limestone house, named Devore Chase. It is notable for its fusion of two styles – Georgian Revival and 18th-century French – which were popular in Kalorama and nearby Sheridan Circle between the 1880s and 1920s. The other sister hired architect Paul Philippe Cret, who reinterpreted the French country house. Cret was well aware that his building would be positioned between Devore Chase and the Lindens nearby; the spirit of both houses is melded in his design for No. 2030.

10 Looking at the house, turn left and follow 24th Street four blocks to the intersection of S Street. At 2340 is the Woodrow Wilson House.

Woodrow Wilson was the only president to remain in Washington after his term in office. He and his wife, Edith, purchased the house in 1921. President Wilson's time here was short-lived, as he died in

WHERE TO EAT

🍽 **BISTROT DU COIN,**
1738 Connecticut Avenue, NW;
Tel: 1-202-234-6969.
Classic bistro fare served in a fun and often loud atmosphere. $$

🍽 **RUSSIA HOUSE,**
1800 Connecticut Avenue, NW;
Tel: 1-202-234-9433.
Eastern European expatriates and more than 90 vodkas make this attractive lounge feel like Moscow on the Potomac. $$

1924. However, Mrs Wilson continued to reside here until her death in 1961. Today, this house is a property of the National Trust for Historic Preservation and is operated as an historic museum. The interiors have been maintained exactly as they were at the time of Wilson's death.
WOODROW WILSON HOUSE;
TUE–SUN 10–4; www.woodrowwilsonhouse.org

11 To get back to Dupont Circle Metro station, exit the Woodrow Wilson House, turn right and proceed along S Street. At the intersection of 22nd Street, NW, turn right and walk down the Decatur Terrace Steps. Walk one block to the intersection of R Street, NW. Turn left onto R Street. Turn right at the intersection of 21st Street, NW. Walk two blocks along 21st Street to the intersection of Q Street, NW. The station is located at the intersection of Q and 20th Streets, NW.

Duke Ellington's Washington

Until the 1920s, Washington could claim the largest urban African-American population in the US. The U Street area was its heart and soul.

Jazz composer, pianist and conductor Edward Kennedy 'Duke' Ellington (1899–1974), born in Washington's West End, spent his boyhood in an area of town that was populated by leading African-American intellectuals of the day and also families of all economic levels. The businesses that they owned and the houses they lived in are featured on this walk. U Street was dubbed 'Black Broadway' for the numerous theatres, cinemas, nightclubs and ballrooms that were frequented by jazz musicians such as Cab Calloway, Pearl Bailey, Jelly Roll Morton and the Duke himself. Along this route, you'll see great jazz venues as well as several establishments that were among the first in the US to welcome a black clientele and the first memorial to African-American soldiers who fought in the US Civil War. Homes occupied by the Ellington family as Duke grew up are also included, along with the corner where rioting started that extinguished the heyday of the area – but only temporarily. U Street has rebounded to become a must-see corridor for out-of-town visitors and locals alike.

From the Metro station exit, turn right and look up at the building directly in front of you. Notice the mural of Duke Ellington by local artist G. Byron Peck. Next, turn left and then cross to the other side of U Street, NW at 13th Street, NW. Proceed to 1215 U Street, the Lincoln Theater.

A recent restoration has returned this theatre to its 1922 glory. When it first opened, the Washington Bee, an African-American newspaper, called it 'perhaps the largest and finest theatre for colored people in the world'. Well-known entertainers performed here and first runs of films were shown. Although the owner of the Lincoln, Abraham Lichtman, was white, he always employed an African-American manager and staff. Behind the theatre once stood the Lincoln Colonnade, a large auditorium that was a favourite venue for sororities, fraternities and other social organizations to hold formal dances.

2 Next door to the Lincoln Theater is Ben's Chili Bowl at 1213 U Street.

Never in their wildest dreams could Ben and Virginia Ali have imagined the beloved place their unassuming chili joint would come to have in the hearts of Washingtonians. The young newlyweds had converted the former Minnehaha Theater into a family-run business in 1958, just as the golden age of U Street was coming to an end. Still, Ben's became the place to be. A decade later, the Alis witnessed and survived the 1968 riots that engulfed the area following the assassination of Martin Luther King. The area fell into decline soon after. Comedian Bill Cosby gave Ben's a much-needed boost when he held a national press conference at the restaurant to celebrate his number-one-rated television series. Five years of construction for the Metro station across the street in the mid 1990s caused business to drop off precipitously again, yet the regulars never stopped coming and Ben's endured. Ben and Virginia have now retired, but their sons, Kalmal and Nizam, continue to greet the legions of local residents who can't get enough of the old school look and unpretentious food.

3 Looking at Ben's, turn right and continue on U Street to the corner of 12th and U Streets, NW. Cross U Street. You will be in front of the True Reformer Building.

DISTANCE I mile (1.6km)

ALLOW I hour

START U Street/Cardozo Metro station (13th Street, NW exit)

FINISH U Street/Cardozo Metro station (13th Street, SE entrance)

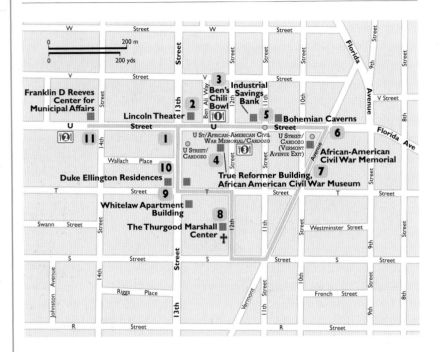

When True Reformer's Hall was constructed in 1902, it was not only one of the tallest buildings north of the city centre, it was also one of the first non-religious structures to be built by an African benevolent organization, the True Reformers. The architect was John A. Lankford (1874–1946), the first black architect to be registered in Washington. Two thousand people could be seated in the second-floor auditorium, which was used for rallies, meetings, dances and theatrical performances. It is also where Duke Ellington played one of his first paid gigs.

4 Cross 12th Street and continue one block to 11th Street, NW. At the intersection of 11th Street, cross U Street and proceed to 2000 11th Street, where there is the Industrial Bank on the corner.

This is the oldest black-owned bank in the city. African-American John Whitelaw Lewis had come to Washington as a

TRUE REFORMER BUILDING

construction worker in the 1890s, but he became the most successful builder and entrepreneur in this part of Washington. By the early 1900s, he had organized a building and loan that was the precursor to Industrial Bank. The Mitchell family took over the bank in 1934 and gave it its name. Founder Jesse H. Mitchell had to train all the bankers himself, because no white banks would hire blacks to gain experience. The Mitchell family continues to operate the bank today.

5 Across 11th Street from Industrial Bank is the Bohemian Caverns nightclub at No. 2003.

John Whitelaw Lewis financed a nightclub on this corner in 1922. Originally called the Caverns, or the Crystal Caverns, it had architecturally rendered stalactites hanging from the ceiling and was a glamorous place that required formal dress. In the 1960s, it was renamed the Bohemian Caverns. Ramsey Lewis and Les McCann both made recordings at this club, and

WHERE TO EAT

🔟 BEN'S CHILI BOWL,
1213 U Street, NW;
Tel: 1-202-667-0909.
Try the chili and also a half-smoke –
a large, spicy hot-dog-like treat that is
one of Washington's specialities. $

🔟 COPPI'S ORGANIC,
1414 U Street, NW;
Tel: 1-202-319-7773.
Brick-oven pizza and light Italian
dishes inspired by the seasons. $$

🔟 DUKEM,
1114 U Street, NW;
Tel: 1-202-667-8735.
The district boasts a large Ethiopian
and Eritrean community. Here is
one of the best spots to sample the
savoury cuisine of those countries. $

'Cannonball' Adderly, Miles Davis and
John Coltrane have all performed here.

6 Looking at Bohemian Caverns
on 11th Street, turn left onto U
Street and proceed one block to the
intersection of 10th and U Streets,
NW. Cross U Street and walk across
the small plaza to the African-American
Civil War Memorial.

The only national memorial to honour
black soldiers who fought in the US Civil
War (1861–65), this bronze sculpture,
The Spirit of Freedom, depicts Freedom as
a woman with her eyes closed and hands
over her chest. On the interior of the
arc is an extended family being protected
by soldiers. The 28,000 names carved
on the wall list the 'US Colored Troops'
and their white officers. During the US
Civil War, greater U Street was the site
of major military encampments that
became safe havens for freed men fleeing
the South. Make sure to stop in at the
memorial's Visitors Center, which is
located in the True Reformer Building
at 12th and U Streets.

7 Leave the memorial, heading towards
the rear, and walk along Vermont
Avenue, NW until you reach the
intersection of S Street, NW. Turn right
onto S Street and then turn right again
onto 12th Street, NW. Stand in front of
No. 1816, which will be on your left.

The first YMCA to provide services to
African-Americans was founded here
in 1853 by Anthony Bowen, a former
slave who had become a civic leader. The
building was completed in 1912. It had
spacious rooms for reading and recreation
as well as a gym, a swimming pool, three
floors of dormitory rooms, a dining room
and a pool room. It was a vital community
centre for African-Americans across the
city. Recently restored, it is now occupied
by a social service and community centre.

8 Follow 12th Street to the
intersection of T Street, NW. Turn
left onto T Street, walking one block
to 13th Street, NW. At the corner
of 13th and T Streets is the Whitelaw
apartment building.

Between 1919 and the 1940s, this cream-coloured brick building was the only first-class hotel open to blacks. John Whitelaw Lewis developed the property in 1919, bestowing his name on the finished product, which had been designed and constructed entirely by African-Americans. After Duke Ellington moved to New York City, he would stay at the Whitelaw when performing in Washington, as did musician Cab Calloway and heavyweight boxer Joe Louis. The Whitelaw was elegant, with potted palms and rich carpets in its lobby and an elegant dining room and ballroom. However, desegregation in the 1950s meant that all Washington hotels were open to blacks and the Whitelaw fell into disrepair. By the 1980s, it had been condemned by the government and abandoned: a tree grew through its roof and a fire caused major damage. Happily, the entire structure was restored between 1991 and 1992 and was made into an apartment building.

9 Cross T Street and continue on 13th Street. Look for No. 1805 on the right side of the street and No. 1816 on the left.

These two houses are where Duke Ellington lived as a teenager, when he was beginning to play with local bands. He moved to this area when he was seven years old. His father, known as 'J.E.', was an elegant man who worked as a butler to a socially prominent Washington family. His son grew up exposed to a refined life and manners. In fact, neighbours marvelled at the young man's politeness and stylish dress, a comportment that Ellington maintained throughout his life. His childhood musical influences included the sacred music he heard at church and the popular music played at local clubs, dance halls and pool halls. Ellington once joked that he had two very different sets of education: one in school and one in the pool hall.

10 Continue on 13th Street back to U Street. Turn left onto U Street and proceed one block to the intersection of U and 14th Streets, NW. On the corner to the left is the Franklin D. Reeves Center for Municipal Affairs.

When Dr Martin Luther King was assassinated in April 1968, riots broke out on this site; they raged for three days and destroyed much of the property on 14th and U Streets. The Reeves Center, an initiative of Mayor Marion Barry, was constructed in 1986 to spark an economic revival that had eluded U Street since the three days of violence. Franklin Reeves, the building's namesake, was a well-known local attorney. The project had special meaning for the centre's designer, architect Paul Devrouax. He had stood on the exact corner in 1968 armed with a rifle as a member of the National Guard sent to protect the area during the riots.

11 To return to U Street/Cardozo Metro, cross 14th Street and follow U Street back to the corner of 13th and U Streets. The entrance to the station is on the southeast corner.

Gracious Homes and Vibrant Streets

Discover one of Washington's most dynamic, pedestrian-friendly residential district, with its lavish 19th-century architecture.

Dupont Circle evolved from a barren wilderness to Washington's most fashionable address at the close of the 19th century. The mansions and elegant terraces remain, many of which are still family houses. Others accommodate museums, bed and breakfasts, embassies or non-profit organizations. This is a cosmopolitan area, where something is always happening, morning, noon and night thanks to the abundance of shops, cafes, bars, restaurants and a bookshop that stays open 24 hours at the weekend. The year-round farmers' market, held on Sundays, is a highlight. Stop by the namesake circle to observe chess players devising a strategy for their next move and bicycle messengers convening for a casual end-of-the-day conference. Wander down one of the residential streets past stunning terraced houses, pausing to admire their lushly planted gardens. The Dupont Circle area has traditionally been a centre of Washington's gay and lesbian community. Each June, the area plays host to Capital Pride, a week of parades, pageants and happy hours. This walk is best taken at a weekend.

From the Metro station, cross 19th Street, NW and then turn onto the one-block-long Sunderland Place, NW. At the intersection of Sunderland Place and New Hampshire Avenue, NW is No. 1307 New Hampshire Avenue.

German immigrant Christian Heurich finished building this residence in 1894 with profits made from his highly successful brewery. The company slogan was 'Beer recommended for family use by Physicians in General'. Heurich, at least, must have benefited from following his own advice, because he was still actively managing the business when he died at age 102. The Heurich family inhabited the house until 1955, when they transferred the deeds to the Historical Society of Washington, DC. After moving its headquarters to Mount Vernon Square, the Historical Society sold the house back to descendants of Christian Heurich. The Brewmaster's Castle, as the house is known today, offers tours of the interior, which has been preserved. The breakfast room walls are covered with murals depicting the virtues of beer drinking.

2 Follow New Hampshire Avenue towards the fountain you can see on Dupont Circle.

During Washington's US Civil War years (1861–65), this piece of land was as remote as you could find. That's hard to imagine, given its vitality today. Not until the 1870s did development arrive in the form of wealthy captains of industry and their families, eager to make their mark

in high society. Two of the mansions they built on the circle remain, one at No. 5 Dupont Circle and one at No. 1801 Massachusetts Avenue, just off the circle itself. The fountain in the centre of the circle commemorates the eponymous Rear Admiral Samuel Francis du Pont (1803–65), a hero of the US Civil War. Dupont Circle plays host to one of the city's most fascinating pedestrian thoroughfares, day or night. On Sundays, visit the farmers' market at 20th Street and Massachusetts Avenue, NW.

3 Exit Dupont Circle at Massachusetts Avenue near P Street, NW. You'll first pass the Sulgrave Club, which has its headquarters in the Gilded Age mansion at No. 1801 Massachusetts Avenue. Continue to the intersection of Massachusetts Avenue and 18th Street, NW. The National Trust for Historic Preservation is at No. 1785 Massachusetts Avenue.

Jules Henri de Sibour was the architect of choice for many moneyed families who desired a 'party palace' in the nation's capital. In 1917, he received a commission from millionaire Stanley McCormick to create 'the most luxurious apartment building in Washington'. The finished building contained just one unit per floor with only six apartments in total. Its exterior resembles those found on residential buildings in Paris, especially the mansard roof, wrought-iron balcony and rusticated first floor. Washington élites such as Lord Joseph Duveen and Andrew Mellon were both residents.

DISTANCE 1 mile (1.6km)

ALLOW 1.5 hours (more with museum visit)

START Dupont Circle Metro station (Dupont South exit)

FINISH Dupont Circle Metro station (Q Street entrance)

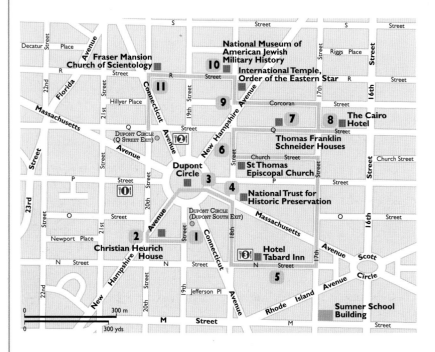

Duveen, an international art dealer, filled his space with an astounding collection of Old Masters art and offered neighbour Mellon the key, thus enabling him to peruse at his leisure. Mellon eventually bought about $21 million worth of paintings and sculptures, donating the collection to the US as the National Gallery of Art (see Walks 5 and 18).

4 Cross Massachusetts Avenue to 18th Street, following it one block to N Street, NW. Turn left onto N Street and proceed to the middle of the block. On the left side is No. 1739.

A place of respite for the pilgrims in Geoffrey Chaucer's *The Canterbury Tales* is the namesake for the Hotel Tabard Inn. Washington residents return again and again for drinks in front of the fireplace or brunch on the garden patio. Legions of out-of-towners wouldn't dream of staying anywhere else. No rooms are alike and the décor throughout is eccentric and homey. Vladimir Lenin watches as you climb the stairs to your room. There's no lift, no room service and no television. But there's no more personable place to sleep or eat in the city. Make sure to try the Inn's signature Route 11 potato chips, which are available at the front desk and in the bar.

5 Follow N Street to the end of the block. At this intersection, turn left onto 17th Street, NW. You'll walk through a restaurant corridor that draws crowds to the al fresco dining tables on fair-weather weekends. At Church Street, NW turn left. Past the modest terraced houses and the Church Street Theater building is the entrance to St Thomas Episcopal Church at 1772 Church Street, NW.

In August 1970, the grand Gothic-style, cruciform church that had been built on this site in 1899 was destroyed by fire. An arsonist was responsible for the blaze but was never caught. The St Thomas vestry voted to remain in the same location – the footprint of the old church was converted to a park, and the Parish Hall (which did not burn) was turned into the worship space used by the church today. At the turn of the 20th century, St Thomas' was a high-society church, attended by the élite who lived in the nearby mansions. However, by the 1960s both the church and the area shed that aristocratic identity and became home to a new population of artists, hippies and activists. The parish became involved in social justice and civil rights, an emphasis its membership maintains to this day.

WHERE TO EAT

⦿ AL TIRAMISU,
2014 P Street, NW;
Tel: 1-202-467-4466.
This cosy Italian restaurant offers great service and truly delicious pasta. $$

⦿ KRAMERBOOKS & AFTERWORDS CAFÉ,
1517 Connecticut Avenue, NW;
Tel: 1-202-387-1400.
Local colour in all its glory, open 24 hours at weekends. Casual dishes and luscious desserts. $

⦿ HOTEL TABARD INN,
1739 N Street, NW;
Tel: 1-202-331-8528.
Even if you don't stop in for a meal at the lovely restaurant, have a drink and a nibble in the bar – there's nothing better on a chilly winter's day in Washington. $$$

6 Turn right onto 18th Street and then right onto Q Street, NW. This is one of the most beautiful residential blocks in Washington.

The varied textures and hues of the stone used in the construction of these terraced houses are particularly magnificent to behold. Many of the houses were designed by Thomas Franklin Schneider, one of Washington's master architect-developers during the late 19th century.

7 At the end of the block, cross 17th Street and continue to No. 1615 Q Street, the tallest building in the city.

Once a fashionable hotel and now an apartment building, the Cairo, designed by Thomas F. Schneider and completed in 1894, is the reason Washington has a building height limit. Even before it was completed, neighbours were protesting about its 160-ft (49-m) rise into the sky. Using the rationale that the city fire service's ladders could not reach that high to extinguish a fire, they successfully lobbied Washington's Board of Commissioners to limit the height of subsequent buildings. A variation of this law continues – as does the debate about whether the law should be abolished

or left untouched. One wonders what Schneider would think of the role his innovative building has played in the evolution of the nation's capital skyline. No doubt the condition of the building in the 1960s would have caused him deep distress, its decline all but complete. However, a 1976 renovation restored some of the Cairo's former glory. Today, the building still soars above all others in Dupont Circle.

8 Double back to 17th Street. Turn right and continue one block to Corcoran Street, NW. Turn left and enjoy the walk down one of the first streets in Dupont Circle to be rehabilitated following the area's decline in the late 1960s. The gas lamps and outdoor artwork are a playful mix of period and contemporary elements. At the intersection of New Hampshire Avenue, NW, where Corcoran and 18th Streets and New Hampshire Avenue meet, you'll find yourself standing in front of the International Order of the Eastern Star headquarters.

No. 1618 New Hampshire Avenue was built to be the home of Diplomat Perry Belmont in 1909. He hired a French architect, who laid out the $1.5 million house in a French manner: the bedrooms were on the ground floor and the main public rooms on the first floor, known as a piano nobile. The piano nobile is the principal floor of a large house that has been elevated to afford views and, more practically, to avoid damp. Belmont sold the house during the Great Depression in the early 1930s to the Order of the Eastern Star, a benevolent organization founded in 1850 by freemason, lawyer and educator Rob Morris. The organization is based on teachings from the Bible but is open to both men and women of all monotheistic faiths. The sale was made with the stipulation that the Right Worthy Grand Secretary of the Eastern Star must live in the house. The emblem of the Order is the five-pointed Star of Bethlehem, which you can see on the fence enclosing the grounds.

9 Turn right onto 18th Street and then left onto R Street, NW. Almost immediately on the right is No. 1811.

Although most of the best-known Jewish historical sites are located in Washington's Chinatown, one aspect of the national Jewish identity can be found here, quietly tucked away in Dupont Circle. The National Museum of American Jewish Military History chronicles the contributions of the men and women of the Jewish faith who have served in the US Armed Forces.

NATIONAL MUSEUM OF AMERICAN JEWISH MILITARY HISTORY;
MON–FRI 9–5; www.nmajmh.org

10 Continue along R Street until you reach the intersection of R and 20th Streets, NW.

The ornate building on the corner was originally built in 1898 for George S. Fraser, a New York merchant. Much of the mansion's grandeur has been restored. If you don't mind being proselytized by members of the Church of Scientology, go inside and look at the hand-carved wood panelling decorating many of the rooms. Scientology was founded in Washington by L. Ron Hubbard in the 1950s. He selected the Fraser mansion building to house what is known as the Founding Church. Public awareness of Scientology has increased as a result of celebrity members such as Tom Cruise.

11 To end the walk, cross 20th Street and Connecticut Avenue and then turn left back onto 20th Street. Follow it for one block until you come to the Q Street entrance of the Dupont Circle Metro station.

Grandes Dames
of Embassy Row

**At the turn of the 20th century, a handful of remarkable wealthy women
made a name for themselves on Massachusetts Avenue.**

The 1888 edition of *Picturesque Washington* estimated that about one-sixth of
Washington's population resided in the city only in winter, during the 'social
season'. Washington Episcopal Bishop Henry Y. Satterlee denounced them from
the pulpit in 1904, asking 'whether the material advantages that they bring are any
compensation for the atmosphere of careless irresponsibility which they create'.
From the late 1870s until the Great Depression, northwest Washington became
home to the nouveau riche who had been successful in industry, agriculture and
finance. Unacceptable in the established high societies of Philadelphia and New
York, they flocked to Washington and built extravagant residences. On this walk,
you'll meet a group of women from this era. For some, the burden of wealth
proved too heavy; others charted a steady course to make enduring contributions
to the city. Today, most of their former homes house embassies or private clubs,
and the avenue on which they stand has been named Embassy Row.

1 Leave Dupont Circle (Dupont South exit) Metro station, turn right onto 19th Street, NW. Do not cross the street onto Dupont Circle. Instead, turn right again, crossing Connecticut Avenue, NW. The next block will be Massachusetts Avenue, NW. Cross it and then turn right to stand in front of No. 1801.

Like many of their contemporaries, Henry and Martha Wadsworth spent the winter social season in Washington. For Martha, talented amateur pianist and accomplished horsewoman, the height of the experience was the season's finale. She frequently organized an 800-mile (1,285-km) trek on horseback from Washington to her estate in the Genesee Valley of western New York State. Her friends joined Martha on horseback and travelled over several weeks, enjoying picnics, parties and overnight stays at local inns and private houses. The household staff, the luggage and the family dogs travelled ahead by train and car in order to prepare for their mistress' arrival. Around the time of World War I, Washington's extravagant social scene began to fade and in 1917 the couple stopped using the house. It sat empty for many years until 1932, when Martha Wadsworth's old friend and neighbour, Mabel Boardman, organized a group of socially prominent women to purchase the house and convert it to a women's club. The founders named it Sulgrave Club, in honour of George Washington's ancestral home, Sulgrave Manor.

2 P Street, NW runs behind the Sulgrave Club. Cross it and stand in front of the large white mansion at 15 Dupont Circle now known as the Washington Club.

In 1950, another women's club purchased this residence known as the Patterson House. Constructed in 1901, it was the scene of many a lavish society event hosted by Mr and Mrs Robert Patterson, its original owners. Mrs Patterson maintained a staff of 10 to 15 servants who, until World War I, wore full livery. This refined atmosphere may be why Charles A. Lindbergh stayed at the house while receiving a hero's welcome in Washington following his transatlantic flight, and President and Mrs Calvin Coolidge used the Patterson while the White House was being refurbished. Yet the most notable occupant of the house was actually the Patterson daughter, known as Cissy. After adhering to the dictates of high society, in which she married (and divorced) a European count, Cissy embarked on life as a wealthy, well-connected single woman. Her friend, renowned newspaper publisher William Randolph Hearst (1863–1951), encouraged her to take up journalism, eventually appointing her editor of the *Washington Herald*. By 1942, Patterson had taken over both the *Washington Times* and the *Washington Herald*. The two papers were combined to form the *Washington Times-Herald*, Cissy became its editor, and she increased her reputation as one of the most influential Washingtonians of her day.

OPPOSITE: ONCE A FAMILY HOME, 2020 MASSACHUSETTS AVENUE IS NOW THE INDONESIAN EMBASSY

DISTANCE 1 mile (1.6km)

ALLOW 1.5 hours (more with museum visits)

START Dupont Circle Metro station (Dupont South exit)

FINISH Dupont Circle Metro station (Q Street entrance)

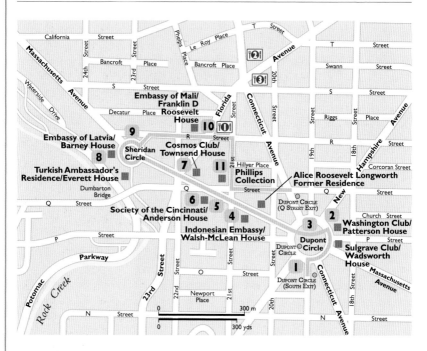

3 Cross the street onto Dupont Circle itself. Walk past the fountain and cross to the other side, exiting the circle by crossing the street onto Massachusetts Avenue. Walk about one block to No. 2009 on the right.

Of his daughter Alice, Theodore Roosevelt (26th president of the US, 1901–09) once observed, 'I can either run the country or I can control Alice. I cannot possibly do both.' Roosevelt's oldest child was one of the most rambunctious,

freewheeling children ever to roam the White House. By the time she reached adulthood, Alice had honed her capacity to shock and flout convention. The house at 2009 Massachusetts Avenue was her home following the death of her husband, Republican speaker of the House Nicholas Longworth. It became a salon, drawing politicians, writers, film stars – anyone who kept Alice entertained. When she died in 1980 at age 96, Alice was declared to be 'the other Washington monument'.

4 Continue along Massachusetts Avenue, noting No. 2020 across the street, now the Indonesian Embassy.

Father Struck It Rich was the title of the memoir written by Evalyn Walsh McLean, who grew up in this mansion and later inherited it from her parents. Her father, Thomas Walsh, made his fortune in Colorado gold mines. His daughter was the quintessential 'poor little rich girl', who embraced the highlife with gusto. In 1908, Evalyn eloped, against her family's advice, with the handsome heir to the *Washington Post* fortune, Edward ('Ned') Beale McLean. In 1911, the couple purchased the Hope Diamond, a 45-carat deep blue stone, which was said to be cursed. Although her friends urged her to keep the diamond concealed, Evalyn often wore it in public. Was she tempting fate? The effects of lifelong alcoholism led to an early death for her estranged husband; her son, Vinson, died from injuries in a car accident at age nine; her daughter, Emily, suffered a drug overdose; and Evalyn herself died at age 60 of pneumonia. Her unlucky jewel is now on display in the Smithsonian Museum of Natural History.

5 Remain on Massachusetts Avenue, crossing 21st Street, NW. Across the street from the statue of Mohandas Gandhi is 2118 Massachusetts Avenue, the Society of the Cincinnati.

In 1896, while serving at the US Embassy in Rome, Larz Anderson met Isabel Weld Perkins, a young debutante from

WHERE TO EAT

🍽 **RESTAURANT NORA,**
2132 Florida Avenue, NW;
Tel: 1-202-462-5143.
Deliciously prepared organic produce, meats and dairy products served in a former grocery store. $$$

🍽 **BUCA DI BEPPO,**
1825 Connecticut Avenue, NW;
Tel: 1-202-232-8466.
Southern Italian culinary legacy in all its kitschy American glory. $$

🍽 **THAIPHOON,**
2011 S Street, NW;
Tel: 1-202-667-3505.
Thai noodle dishes, curries and soups. $$

Boston. At age five, Isabel had inherited 17 million dollars from her grandfather, William Fletcher Weld, making her the wealthiest woman in the world. She and Larz were married and embarked on a life of luxury combined with public service and adventure. They travelled widely across the world, becoming among the first Westerners to visit countries such as Tibet and Nepal. When she became a widow, Isabel deeded this property and its contents to the Society of the Cincinnati – a patriotic organization of which Larz had been a lifelong member – for use as a headquarters and a museum.
SOCIETY OF THE CINCINNATI;
TUE–SAT 1–4; www.societyofthecincinnati.org

6 Continue along Massachusetts Avenue until you reach No. 2121, the Cosmos Club.

The first house on this site was built in 1871 by a property speculator. In 1900, Richard Townsend, his wife Mary and their daughter Mathilde moved here from Lafayette Square. Although Mrs Townsend disliked the house, a childhood superstition led her to believe that evil would befall her if she ever lived in a new house, and she could not bring herself to tear down the original. Instead, the Townsends built around the old edifice, incorporating it into a lavish mansion. Mrs Townsend rested easy at first, but her anxiety levels must have risen when, a year after moving into the house, Richard fell from a horse, fractured his skull and died. She seems to have coped by continuing to entertain in grand style: her expenses for social events often exceeded $240,000 a year. In 1950, the property became the private Cosmos Club, where professionals in the arts and sciences meet to exchange ideas.

7 Cross Florida Avenue, NW and stay on Massachusetts Avenue until you reach Sheridan Circle. Cross Massachusetts Avenue in front of the Greek ambassador's residence at No. 2221. Turn right and follow the road to 23rd Street, NW. Almost directly across 23rd Street is No. 1606, the Turkish ambassador's residence. Notice the charming portrait of Isabel Anderson (see Step 5) concealed in the red police phone box on 23rd Street.

The money that paid for this – one of the most spectacular homes on Embassy Row – came from the crimped bottle cap for soda pop and beer bottles, invented by Edward H. Everett. He gave architect George Oakley Totten free rein in design, insisting cost was of no concern. The resulting home continues to be used today for grand social functions by the Turkish ambassador. Everett's second wife was operatic soprano Grace Burnap. Together, they hosted 'Evenings with Music', accommodating several hundred guests. Attendance at one party in the 1930s was estimated at 3,000. The *Washington Sunday Star* reported, 'footmen in mulberry livery with white silk stockings and pumps with silver buckles were everywhere".

8 Return to Sheridan Circle and turn left. The Spanish Mission-style building at 2306 Massachusetts Avenue is the Latvian Embassy.

When she built this relatively modest home on Sheridan Circle in 1901, free-spirited Alice Pike Barney made an important contribution to Washington's art scene. The building served as her home, her art studio and Washington's ad hoc cultural centre, where Alice hosted theatrical productions and art exhibitions. She had been inspired by years spent in France studying painting, much to the disapproval of her husband, Albert. Alice ignored his protests, spending less time with him and more time with her artist companions and two daughters. In 1901, she presented her first solo exhibition at the Corcoran Gallery of Art, in

ABOVE: HEADQUARTERS AND MUSEUM OF THE SOCIETY OF THE CINCINNATI, A US PATRIOTIC ORGANIZATION

Washington. During World War I, Alice Barney convinced Congress to fund construction of the National Sylvan Theater in the grounds of the Washington Monument. She also raised money for Neighborhood House, which offered social services to immigrants in southwest Washington. Today, three branches of what is now called the Barney Neighborhood House continue to provide social services in the city.

9 Continue around Sheridan Circle, crossing Massachusetts Avenue and proceeding along R Street, NW. Follow R Street across 22nd Street and then look for No. 2133, the Embassy of Mali.

Franklin and Eleanor Roosevelt lived at this address from 1917 to 1920, while Roosevelt was assistant secretary of the navy. In autumn 1918, Eleanor discovered that her husband was having an affair with her social secretary, Lucy Mercer. Eleanor offered Franklin a divorce, yet partly because divorce was considered a disgrace in their social circle and partly because it would have badly damaged his political career, Franklin asked to stay married and agreed never to see Lucy again. The incident profoundly altered their relationship and was a major factor in Eleanor's search for friendship and fulfilment in social and political activism independent of her spouse. Despite their parallel lives, however, by the time the Roosevelts reached the White House in 1933, they were able to function highly effectively, Eleanor playing an integral role in the Roosevelt presidency.

10 Follow R Street across Florida Avenue. Note Restaurant Nora as you continue on R Street. Chef Nora Pouillon is one of the grand dames of the Washington culinary scene, having converted a grocery store into one of the city's best restaurants. At the intersection of 21st Street, NW, turn right, cross R Street and proceed on 21st Street to the Phillips Collection, which will be on the right.

Artist Marjorie Acker married Duncan Phillips in 1921 and resided with her husband on the third floor of his family's spacious house. That same year they opened the main floor to the public as the Phillips Collection, the first museum of modern art in the US, comprising art acquired by Duncan and (later) Marjorie. When the collection outgrew this space, the Phillips made their entire house into a museum, building a new house for themselves in northwest Washington. At their new home, the couple acquired paintings on loan, hung them and 'tested' them. If after two months they were still excited about the piece, they bought it and sent it to the Phillips Collection. That artwork can be viewed today, as well as a number of Marjorie's paintings.

THE PHILLIPS COLLECTION; TUE–SAT 10–5, THU 10–8:30, SUN 11–6; www.phillipscollection.org

11 From the Phillips Collection, turn right. Walk to the end of the block to the intersection of Q Street, NW. Turn left onto Q Street. The Metro station is at the end of the block.

OPPOSITE: THE PHILLIPS COLLECTION ART GALLERY, THE FIRST MUSEUM OF MODERN ART IN THE US

The Best-kept Smithsonian Secrets

If you enjoy exquisite gallery space, rare treasures, appealing outdoor viewing areas and unexpected treats, this is the walk for you.

Take this walk on a hot, sultry day when the cool, quiet spaces will provide much-needed relief. The most popular (and usually most crowded) of the Smithsonian museums – the National Air and Space Museum, the National Museum of Natural History, and the National Museum of American History – are more than worthy of repeat visits. Consider, though, that the Smithsonian Institution encompasses 19 museums, nine of which can be found along the National Mall. This walk is an opportunity to explore that cultural bounty via less familiar venues. The route travels inside serenely beautiful gallery space located both above and below ground, through lush Victorian-era gardens as well as inside two sculpture gardens. Every stop has been selected to reveal an unusual or little-known aspect of the Smithsonian experience. It's a rewarding way to acquaint yourself with some of the best painting, sculpture and landscape architecture in Washington in a short period of time and without the crowds.

After leaving Smithsonian Metro station by the Mall exit, turn right, crossing Jefferson Drive, SW, and approach the Italian Renaissance-style building to your left.

The Freer Gallery of Art, founded by Charles Lang Freer (1854–1919), houses a world-renowned collection of art from China, Japan, Korea and Southeast Asia. Not your cup of tea? Enter nonetheless to enjoy the elegant museum building and its sublime interior courtyard. Also, make your way back to the gallery that houses the lavishly ornate Peacock Room. This dining room was once part of a London townhouse owned by Frederick R. Leyland, a wealthy ship owner from Liverpool, UK. He commissioned the US artist James McNeill Whistler (1834–1903) to decorate the room, but unfortunately Leyland was not happy with the result and arguments ensued. Freer purchased the Peacock Room in 1904, and it was dismantled and taken to his house in Detroit. After his death it was taken to the Freer Gallery in Washington.

FREER GALLERY OF ART;

DAILY 10–5.30; www.asia.si.edu

2 From outside the Freer Gallery, turn right and walk over to the charming, leaf-topped kiosk next door.

Just because many who enter this building appear to be Smithsonian employees doesn't mean the general public is not welcome. Indeed, the S. Dillon Ripley Center houses gallery space expressly

for visitors, and there are often exhibits covering a particular theme, event or American ethnic group. A peek inside also affords you the chance to see how the Smithsonian Institution administration functions behind the scenes. Its popular Smithsonian Associates program is based here, as well the Traveling Exhibition Service. For those with youngsters, check the schedule of events for the Discovery Theater. Dillon Ripley (1913–2001), the centre's namesake, was secretary of the Smithsonian Institution from 1964 to 1984.

S. DILLON RIPLEY CENTER;

DAILY 10–5.30; www.si.edu/ripley

WHERE TO EAT

🔟 GARDEN CAFÉ,
National Gallery of Art
(West Building, Ground floor),
7th Street and Constitution
Avenue, NW;
Tel: 1-202-712-7454.
An indoor garden setting complements the artful menu that is often inspired by whatever major exhibition is on view. $$

🔟 MITSITAM CAFÉ,
National Museum of the American Indian,
4th Street and Independence
Avenue, SW;
Tel: 1-202-633-1000.
Imaginative and delicious native foods from the major US regions, presented with a contemporary twist. $$

OPPOSITE: THE CIRCULAR CEILING AT THE NATIONAL MUSEUM OF THE AMERICAN INDIAN

DISTANCE **0.5 mile (0.8km)**

ALLOW **I hour (more with museum visits)**

START **Smithsonian Metro station (Mall exit)**

FINISH **Archives-Navy Memorial Metro station**

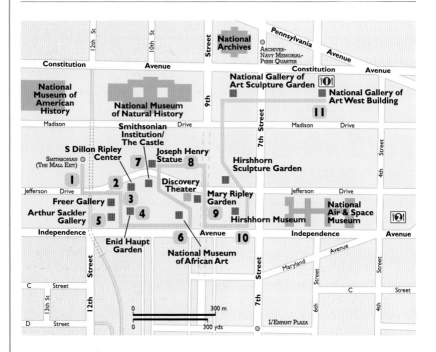

3 Exit the Ripley Center and turn right into the Enid Haupt Garden.

S. Dillon Ripley conceived this quadrangle to accommodate museum space. During Ripley's tenure, Dr Arthur M. Sackler pledged part of his enormous collection of Asian and Near Eastern art, but the Smithsonian had nowhere to display it. Likewise, the Museum of African Art had outgrown its terraced-house quarters on Capitol Hill. In 1982, Congress appropriated the funds to construct the two museums. They are underground, so are not visible from street level, but you can see their entry pavilions on the right and the left. The formal garden atop the museum space was created in 1987 – a gift from New York benefactress Enid Haupt.

4 Follow the garden walk to your right, heading towards the Arthur Sackler Gallery. Notice the Moon Gate Garden located next to the museum's entry pavilion.

Arthur M. Sackler (1913–87) was a New York psychiatrist, medical researcher and publisher who donated 1,000 objects from his personal collection to the Smithsonian in 1982. The building interconnects underground with the Freer Gallery. Next to the Sackler Gallery is an intimate garden with a circle-in-square fountain, based on the Temple of Heaven in Beijing. Two 'moon gates', 9ft (2.7m) high, complete the setting.

ARTHUR SACKLER GALLERY;

DAILY 10–5.30; www.asia.si.edu

5 From the Sackler Gallery, walk across the garden to the National Museum of African Art.

Traditional and contemporary art from the African continent is on display here. A common characteristic of many of the objects is that they were used in everyday life. The museum also offers you the chance to listen to the sounds of Africa in the form of live Radio Africa broadcasts as well as podcasts. Adjacent to the museum building is a series of fountains and canals terminating in a *chadar*, or water wall, inspired by the Moorish Alhambra gardens in Granada, Spain.

NATIONAL MUSEUM OF AFRICAN ART;

DAILY 10–5.30; www.nmafa.si.edu

6 From the museum, follow the path along the garden's parterre towards the Smithsonian Institution entrance. Enter the building and walk through the main hall towards the opposite entrance. To the right of the entrance way is the James Smithson Room.

In 1826, British scientist James Smithson (1765–1829) made out his Last Will and Testament declaring that he would entail his estate to his nephew. If the nephew died without an heir, however, even though Smithson had never visited the US, the money was to go 'to the United States of America, to found at Washington, under the name of the Smithsonian Institution, an establishment for the increase and diffusion of knowledge'. The said nephew died without offspring, and the inheritance – valued at half a million dollars – came to the US. Although he died in Italy, Smithson's remains were eventually brought to the US, where they have rested ever since. What exactly motivated him to make the bequest to the United States remains a mystery.

SMITHSONIAN INSTITUTION/ THE CASTLE;

DAILY 8.30–5.30;

www.si.edu/visit/infocenter/sicastle.htm

ABOVE: THE SMITHSONIAN INSTITUTION'S FIRST BUILDING, POPULARLY KNOWN AS THE CASTLE

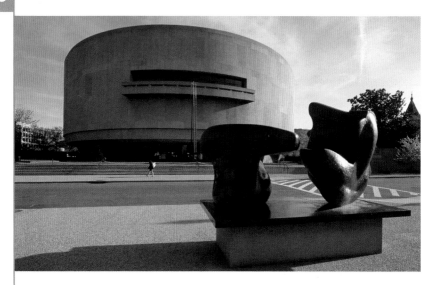

7 **Exit the Castle building, cross Jefferson Drive and walk down the steps. To your immediate right is a statue of a man on a pedestal.**

No doubt a majority of passers-by behold the dignified man standing in front of a building called Smithsonian and identify him as James Smithson. But look closely at the name carved on the pedestal and you will see the inscription 'Joseph Henry'. An eminent American scientist, Joseph Henry (1797–1878) was the first secretary of the Smithsonian Institution and held the position for 34 years. (One of the job's perks was an apartment in the east wing of the Castle.) When he died, such was his stature that the US president, the cabinet, the chief justice and associate justices of the Supreme Court, as well as members of both houses of Congress attended the funeral. US sculptor William W. Story (1819–95) embedded

an electromagnet in the pedestal upon which Henry leans, honouring one of the physicist's primary areas of research.

8 **Climb back up the steps and cross Jefferson Drive again. Turn left and walk along the Castle grounds, passing the festive Arts & Industries Building. Turn right into the Mary Ripley Garden.**

One of the loveliest spots in the city at any time of year, the Mary Ripley Garden was created in 1987 to commemorate the wife of Smithsonian secretary S. Dillon Ripley. Its formal layout, wrought-iron furniture and dense, varied plantings provide a hint of how the National Mall outside once appeared. A 1850s plan proposed by landscape architect Andrew Jackson Downing (1815–52) turned an under-utilized piece of land into a vast Victorian garden complete with flowerbeds, a flower

ABOVE: THE DOUGHNUT-SHAPED HIRSHHORN MUSEUM, CENTRE FOR CONTEMPORARY ART AND CULTURE

meadow and winding carriage paths. The sweeping, open vistas you see today – while included in Washington's original city plan designed in 1791 – were not achieved until the early 20th century.

9 Exit the garden back to Jefferson Drive. Turn right almost immediately onto the grounds of the Hirshhorn Museum. Follow the path around the building, past the main entrance, and then a bit further until you come to a tall sculpture made from aluminium tubes.

There's more to 'Needle Tower' than meets the eye. Notice the stones placed on the ground beneath it. Stand on them and look up to see the familiar, five-pointed shape that resembles the Star of David. The doughnut-shaped Hirshhorn Museum is a centre for contemporary art and culture, presenting exhibits, lectures and films. Erected in 1971, it was constructed on the site of the former Army Medical Museum, which was razed and relocated in order to allow the art collection of industrialist Joseph Hirshhorn to secure a home on the National Mall. Famous for its collection of artefacts and photographs detailing US Civil War medicine, the Army Medical Museum tended to shock the viewing public and, probably for that very reason, was well attended. In fact, the potential loss of the collection to the Hirshhorn building caused such a stir that the exhibits were relocated to the campus of Walter Reed Army Medical Center.

HIRSHHORN MUSEUM;

DAILY 10–5.30; http://hirshhorn.si.edu

10 Continue to follow the path around the Hirshhorn Museum back to Jefferson Drive. Cross Jefferson Drive and follow the steps down into the Hirshhorn Museum Sculpture Garden. Walk through the garden and out of the opposite entrance back onto the National Mall. Walk straight across the Mall towards the National Gallery of Art Sculpture Garden. Walk through and exit at the corner of 7th Street and Constitution Avenue, NW. Cross 7th Street and walk towards the 7th Street entrance of the National Gallery of Art West Building.

The National Gallery of Art exhibits one of the rarest pieces of art in the US: a Leonardo da Vinci. Painted between 1474 and 1478, the double-sided painting Ginevra de' Benci is the only work by this Tuscan master in the US. The young Ginevra was captured on canvas probably around the time of her marriage at age 16, and is currently to be found in Gallery 6.

NATIONAL GALLERY OF ART;

MON–SAT 10–5, SUN 11–6; www.nga.gov

11 To get to the nearest Metro station, leave the gallery's entrance on 7th Street, NW, turn right and proceed to the intersection at Constitution Avenue, crossing the street. Continue on 7th Street to Pennsylvania Avenue, NW. Cross Pennsylvania Avenue and then turn left to cross 7th Street. The entrance to the Archives-Navy Memorial-Penn Quarter Metro station is to the right.

The Kennedys in Georgetown

Fashionable, high-status residents such as the Kennedy family helped to establish Georgetown as the social and political centre of the US capital.

Georgetown continues to enjoy a reputation as the home of the influential élite, but it didn't come by this identity until the 1950s. Prior to that time, it had suffered the vicissitudes of its economy – based first on tobacco trading and then industry – and was a motley area comprised of wealthy merchants, middle-class shopkeepers, free and enslaved African-Americans and poor white immigrants. The Kennedy era in Georgetown coincided with a movement by many connected to the government to live close to the city centre as well as a desire to preserve the area's historic character. The Kennedys conferred a social and political status on Georgetown that had not existed to that point. They marked some of their best times in Washington here as well as a few of the more heartbreaking. This walk pays tribute to those events by visiting homes where the Kennedy family lived, a church where they worshipped, and residences of others impacted by their tenure. Note that all the houses on this route remain private residences.

1 Exiting Foggy Bottom Metro station, turn left and proceed to Washington Circle. Turn left and walk around the circle, exiting onto Pennsylvania Avenue by bearing left. Follow Pennsylvania Avenue to the intersection of 28th Street, NW. At this point the street changes its name to M Street, NW. Follow M Street six blocks to the intersection of M and Potomac Streets, NW. Dean & DeLuca at 3276 M Street will be on the left.

Joel Dean and Giorgio DeLuca opened their first market in SoHo, New York City, in 1977. Since then, Dean & DeLuca has become famous for its bread and cheese, first-rate foods and high-quality cookware and accessories. Outposts of the food emporium can now be found in California's Napa Valley, Kansas City and Charlotte, North Carolina.

2 From Dean & DeLuca, cross M Street, NW and proceed up Potomac Street, NW. At the intersection of N Street, NW turn left. Midway along this block on the left side of the street is 3260 N Street, NW.

While renting this house, built in 1828, John F. Kennedy began his campaign for his seat in the US Senate. In spite of the strong public support for Republican Dwight Eisenhower, Kennedy won what had been a close campaign. While living here, Kennedy attended a dinner party at the home of Georgetown friends, where he met a striking young woman named Jacqueline Bouvier, who was later to become his wife.

3 Continue along N Street, crossing 33rd Street, NW. On your right will be No. 3307.

The William Marbury House was constructed in 1812 and purchased by John F. Kennedy in 1957. He took the deed of the house to the hospital and presented it as a gift to his wife, Jacqueline, who had just given birth to their first child, Caroline. John Kennedy, Jr was also born while they lived here. Mrs Kennedy is reputed to have decorated the house three times during their first year of residence, while her husband focused on winning the presidential campaign of 1960. After his victory, the doorway of this house became instantly recognizable because of the cadre of reporters who waited across the street day and night for word from the president-elect about cabinet appointments and other administration news.

4 Cross the street to 3302 N Street.

One of the bronze plaques on the east side of this house commemorates Helen Montgomery. When her neighbour across the street was elected US President, Montgomery took pity on the constant swarm of news reporters standing in the cold waiting for a story to break, so she and her father, Charles, offered food, a warm room and use of the telephone to these journalists. In appreciation, John F. Kennedy himself presented the plaque to Miss Montgomery on Inauguration Day, 1961. She died in 1975.

OPPOSITE: THE FEDERAL-STYLE TOWNHOUSES OF COX'S ROW IN GEORGETOWN

DISTANCE **3.5 miles (5.6km)**

ALLOW **3 hours**

START **Foggy Bottom Metro station**

FINISH **Foggy Bottom Metro station**

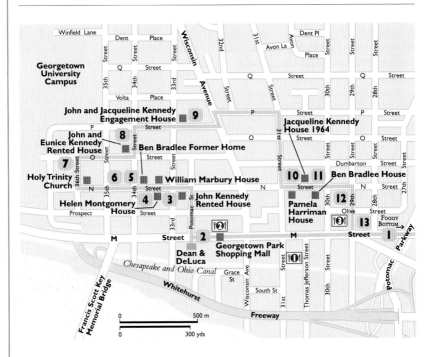

5 Just a little further on N Street on the right is No. 3321, former home of Ben Bradlee.

Newsweek magazine's Washington correspondent Ben Bradlee enjoyed a close friendship with Senator John F. Kennedy. The two first met when wheeling their infant children around in their prams. Bradlee kept notes of their intimate conversations, with Kennedy's knowledge, and these records became the basis for a behind-the-scenes book revealing the human side of the JFK presidency published by Bradlee following Kennedy's death. *Conversations with Kennedy* was described as providing an insight into what Kennedy was really like, although Mrs Kennedy apparently objected to the book's profanity and ended the friendship with the Bradlees. Another difficult moment in the Bradlee–Kennedy relationship took place in 1964, when Bradlee's sister-in-law, Mary Pinchot Meyer, was found murdered on the C & O Canal towpath.

Meyer had been a friend of Jacqueline Kennedy, and a sensational diary she left at the little studio apartment above Bradlee's N Street home indicated she had also been a lover of John F. Kennedy. Her murder was never solved.

6 Follow N Street across 34th and 35th Streets, NW. Stop in front of the Holy Trinity Church, Chapel of St Ignatius Loyola, at No. 3515.

The Kennedy family often worshipped at Holy Trinity Church. This building, now called St Ignatius Chapel, was the original church, constructed in 1794. The present sanctuary is around the corner, on 36th Street, by the Holy Trinity School. This is a Jesuit parish that has always enjoyed a close relationship with its institution neighbour, Georgetown University.

7 Turn right onto 36th Street, NW. At the intersection of 36th and O Streets, NW you will get a glimpse of the Georgetown University campus. Turn right onto O Street, cross 35th Street and take the next turn left onto 34th Street. Look for 1400 34th Street, which will be on your left.

Senator John F. Kennedy rented this house with his sister, Eunice, who gave up her share of the rent when she became engaged to Sergeant Shriver. JFK then moved to a smaller house at 3271 P Street, NW in the eastern part of Georgetown. He did not yet know that he would soon be married, just four months after Eunice. Eunice

WHERE TO EAT

🍴 CAFÉ LA RUCHE,
1039 31st Street, NW;
Tel: 1-202-965-2684.
Casual bistro near the C & O Canal, with outdoor garden seating and hard-to-resist desserts. $

🍴 CLYDE'S OF GEORGETOWN,
3236 M Street, NW;
Tel: 1-202-333-9180.
Washington institution that continues to please due to its extensive menu of sandwiches, soups, salads, pasta, meat and fish dishes. $$

🍴 MENDOCINO GRILLE,
2917 M Street, NW;
Tel: 1-202-333-2912.
Restaurant/wine bar offering seasonable, sustainable ingredients along with an award-winning wine list starring selections from California and the northwest. $$$

Kennedy Shriver's daughter, Maria, became the wife of actor–politician Arnold Schwarzenegger.

8 Continue on 34th Street until you reach the intersection of P Street, NW. Turn right onto P Street. Soon after you cross 33rd Street, stop in front of 3271 P Street.

John Kennedy was living in this house when he sent a telegram to a female photographer who was working for

After the assassination of her husband in 1963, Jacqueline Kennedy moved with her children, Caroline and John Jr, from the White House to this temporary residence, where they lived for four months before finding a home of their own. It was offered for their use by Averell Harriman, a business tycoon and Democratic Party stalwart. In 1971, Harriman married Pamela Churchill Hayward (1920–97), an English-born socialite who had been married twice before: first, to Randolph Churchill (Winston Churchill's son), then later to Broadway producer Leland Hayward, with whom she remained until his death. On marrying Harriman and moving to Washington, Pamela quickly became a renowned Georgetown hostess and consummate party-giver. She soon became an influential figure in Washington's Democratic Fellowship and was eventually appointed US Ambassador to France by President Bill Clinton.

the *Washington-Times Herald*. Jacqueline Bouvier was the 'Inquiring Photographer' for the paper and had been sent to London to cover the coronation of Queen Elizabeth. The telegram was Kennedy's proposal of marriage. She accepted, and the two spent many hours here planning their wedding, which took place the following September at Hammersmith Farm, the Newport, Rhode Island estate owned by Jacqueline's family.

9 Walk along P Street, crossing the busy Wisconsin Avenue, NW. Keep on P Street until you get to the intersection of 31st Street, NW, where you will turn right. Follow 31st Street through the intersections of O and Dumbarton Street, NW. When you come to N Street, turn left. Stop in front of 3038 N Street.

10 Cross the street to look at No. 3017.

Known as the Laird-Dunlop House, notable Georgetown residents have lived here since it was built around 1799. One inhabitant was Robert Todd Lincoln (1843–1926), American lawyer and politician and the oldest son of President Abraham Lincoln, who purchased the home in 1915. Its current owners are former *Washington Post* Executive Editor Ben Bradlee and his journalist wife, Sally Quinn.

ABOVE: THE CHAPEL OF ST IGNATIUS LOYOLA, WHERE THE KENNEDYS USED TO WORSHIP

11 Across the street you'll find 3014 N Street.

Built before 1800, this house was once a 19th-century academy for young girls. In 1964, it became the home of the widowed Jacqueline Kennedy. Her attempt to remain in Georgetown, a place she loved, was to no avail. Throngs of curious people camped out on her narrow street night and day, just to catch a glimpse of her. After only 10 months in this house, she moved to New York City.

12 Follow N Street to 29th Street, NW. Turn right and proceed until you reach M Street, NW, the commercial heart of Georgetown.

In this commercial district you can find a variety of eateries and outposts of well-known US retailers such as Kate Spade, Pottery Barn, Urban Outfitters and Banana Republic, to name but a few.

13 To return to Foggy Bottom Metro station, turn left at the intersection of 29th and M Streets. Follow M Street to 28th Street, where it changes its name to Pennsylvania Avenue. Follow Pennsylvania Avenue to Washington Circle, bearing right to walk around the circle. Exit the circle by turning right onto 23rd Street, NW. The station will be on the right, halfway down the block.

ABOVE: 3017 N STREET BECAME HOME TO THE RECENTLY WIDOWED JACQUELINE KENNEDY FOR 10 MONTHS

The Haunted Houses of Lafayette Square

The ghosts and spirits of military heroes, young girls, a tragic slave, First Ladies and a US president fill the well-known enclave of Lafayette Square.

Beneath the political history of the capital city of the US churns a haunted legacy borne from desperate suffering and violent death. A gloomy supernatural cloud hovers darkly over a 7-acre (2.8-hectare) park more accustomed to the purposeful step of civil servants and the carefree gait of visiting high-school students than the restless wanderings of ghosts, forever bound to the place where their death occurred. Start at the first private residence constructed on Lafayette Square, which has been disturbed by the ghost of its first owner almost since the day he died. The spirit of a courageous First Lady is known to revisit her final Washington residence, and when an up-and-coming military officer witnessed a horrific assassination, his Lafayette Square home seemed to fall under a bloody curse. Even the White House has been associated with spooky encounters. You'll conclude the walk at what is considered the most ghost-filled place in Washington, the Octagon House.

From Farragut West's 17th Street exit, step out onto I Street, NW. Turn right and walk to the corner of I Street and Connecticut Avenue, NW. Follow Connecticut Avenue to the end of the block, then cross H Street, NW. You will now be standing in front of the Stephen Decatur House Museum.

A shadowy, amorphous form is said to move out of the front room to the left of the main entrance and make its way towards a door at the back of the house. A man dressed in military garb from the early 19th century has been seen on the stairway. Is he also the source of the horrendous crashing sounds that resonate, seemingly out of nowhere? Many employed at this house museum believe so. Commodore Stephen Decatur and his wife, Susan, built this fine Lafayette Square residence in 1819. It was soon the scene of glittering parties attended by Washington notables. Decatur, the country's naval hero, was one of the most famous men in the US, destined, many assumed, for additional glory. But alas, Decatur's ambition was snuffed out abruptly. On 22 March 1820 he died in this house from wounds received in a duel. His unhappy, frustrated ghost has made its presence known ever since.

STEPHEN DECATUR HOUSE MUSEUM;
MON–FRI 9–5; TEL: 1-202.842.0920;
www.decaturhouse.org

2 Follow the path parallel to H Street, NW across to the other side of the park. At the corner of H Street and Madison Place, NW is a yellow house.

Statesman Daniel Webster assessed First Lady Dolley Madison as 'The only permanent power in Washington, all others are transient'. Beloved and admired, Mrs Madison ushered in an era of elegance at the White House, hosting weekly gatherings that were so vital to the city's social and political life. She was there when, in August 1814, British soldiers invaded the city and set fire to nearly every government building, the White House included. Not one to panic, Mrs Madison ordered her staff to remove as many treasures from the building as possible to prevent them from falling into British hands. Most iconic was a full-length portrait of America's first president, General George Washington, painted by Gilbert Stuart. That it continues to hang in the East Room of the White House is a testament to Dolley Madison's fortitude and courage. After she and President Madison retired from public life, Dolley later found herself back in Lafayette Square, residing in this corner house from 1837 to 1849, where she died at age 81.

143

DISTANCE **0.5 mile (0.8km)**

ALLOW **1 hour (more with site visits)**

START **Farragut West Metro station (17th Street exit)**

FINISH **Farragut West Metro station (18th Street entrance)**

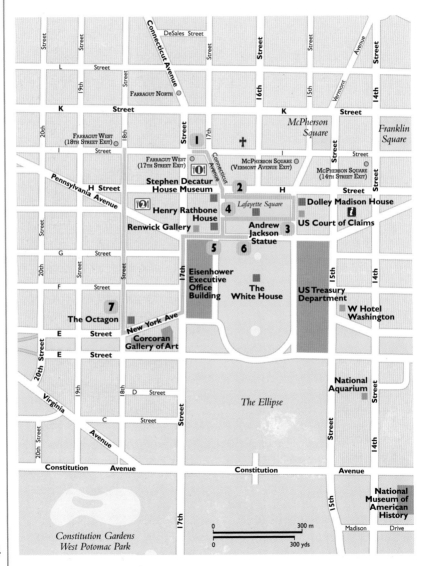

A few years after her death, gentlemen leaving a nearby men's club at night began to notice a woman on the front porch sitting in a rocking chair. Her serene countenance revealed that she was none other than the spirit of their favourite First Lady rocking peacefully in the moonlight.

3 Turn around and walk along the path passing behind the memorial honouring Brigadier General Thaddeus Kosciuszko. Stop at the equestrian statue in the middle of the park.

This is the first equestrian statue ever erected in the US. Placed here in 1853, it commemorates the victories of Major General Andrew Jackson during the War of 1812 fought against Britain. Jackson went on to become the seventh president of the US. When his political career ended, he spent the rest of his life at the Hermitage, his Tennessee estate, where he died in 1845. Twenty years later, lusty laughter was reported in a bedroom located on the third floor of the White House. Those seeking slumber in the Rose Room (or Queen's Bedroom) were often startled by the sound, definitely made by a man yet sounding like it came from nowhere in particular. First Lady Mary Todd Lincoln was one of the first to attribute the laugh to former President Andrew Jackson. What his supernatural association with the bedroom might be is anyone's guess, though the bed slept in by overnight guests was indeed a piece of furniture in the White House when Jackson was president.

4 Looking at the Jackson statue, turn left and follow the path to the other side of the park. Turn left onto Jackson Place and proceed to No. 712.

At the end of the 19th century, many inhabitants of Lafayette Square would have been nervous about walking in front of this house, so convinced were they that a curse enveloped it. Numerous people claimed to hear low, sorrowful moaning coming from within. During the Civil War (1861–65) it had been the home of dashing Major Henry Rathbone. It was the major and his fiancée, Clara Harris, who attended the theatre with President Abraham Lincoln and his wife on the fateful evening of 14 April 1865, when they witnessed Lincoln's assassination. Rathbone, moreover, had been wounded by the president's murderer, John Wilkes Booth, as the former tried to stop the latter from escaping Ford's Theatre. Clara attended her injured betrothed. It was only later that she realized her evening dress was soaked with blood, a gruesome reminder of the evening's tragedy. Rather than dispose of the dress, Clara inexplicably kept it, storing it in a bedroom closet at her family's summer home in upstate New York. She and Henry were married and had children, yet their life together proved doomed. Rathbone never recovered from the guilt he felt at failing to save the president or apprehend his assassin. In 1870, he resigned from the army and set off with his wife and children on a futile quest for a mental cure. His friends and family quietly began to fear for his sanity; Clara

WHERE TO EAT

|O| EQUINOX,
818 Connecticut Avenue, NW;
Tel: 1-202-331-8118.
Chef Todd Gray offers a tempting tasting menu at his modern American restaurant. $$$

|O| KINKEAD'S,
2000 Pennsylvania Avenue, NW;
Tel: 1-202-296-7700.
A mainstay of Washington dining for the simple reason that chef Robert Kinkead specializes in superb seafood. $$$

confided that she wished to leave him but could not bear the disgrace of a divorce. Then, on Christmas Eve morning in 1883, their tragedy found its climactic moment. Rathbone shot Clara and stabbed himself six times. He survived his wounds but spent the remainder of his life institutionalized in Germany. Years later, his son, Henry Riggs Rathbone, returned to the summer house in New York and destroyed the bloody gown, convinced that it had been the source of his parents' doom.

5 Follow Jackson Place to Pennsylvania Avenue, NW. Bearing left, follow the path until you are standing in front of the White House.

Spirits and ghosts abound in America's most famous residence. Random episodes are common – for example,

First Daughters Jenna and Barbara Bush reported opera music coming from the fireplace in their bedroom – as are habitual occurrences, such as the appearance of the ghost of the slain President Abraham Lincoln. First Lady Abigail Adams, the original inhabitant of the house, had her staff dry laundry in the unfinished East Room. Many have reported seeing her spirit moving from the East Room into other parts of the house, her hands outstretched as if she's carrying a load of laundry. Those holding quiet conference in the Blue Room have slowly become aware of violin music playing. Mary Todd Lincoln once said to a friend, 'My, how that Mr Jefferson does play the violin,' referring to America's third president, who used to practise in that room. During a news conference in 1987, President Ronald Reagan shared a story with news reporters about an incident in the Lincoln bedroom, when Lincoln's ghost was sighted sitting on the bed. 'I haven't seen him myself,' said Reagan, 'but every once in a while our little dog Rex will start down that long hall, just glaring as though he's seeing something.' Reagan added that the dog would also bark repeatedly as he stopped in front of the Lincoln bedroom. 'And once I went down and opened the door, and I stepped in and turned around for him to come on. He stood there still barking and growling and then started backing away.'

THE WHITE HOUSE;
GROUP TOURS AVAILABLE (ARRANGEMENTS TO BE MADE IN ADVANCE);
www.whitehouse.gov

6 Looking at the White House, turn right and walk to the end of Pennsylvania Avenue, past the grandiose Executive Office Building on your left. Turn left at 17th Street, NW and proceed to New York Avenue, NW. (The Corcoran Gallery of Art is at the intersection.) Turn right onto New York Avenue and continue to the Octagon, located on the corner of New York Avenue and 18th Street. After viewing the front of the house, turn right and walk a bit up 18th Street, turning right into the garden found at the back of the house. Here is the perfect place to contemplate this building's haunted legacy.

The wealthy, influential Tayloes of Virginia built this home between 1799 and 1801. It became their year-round residence in 1817. Colonel John and Mrs Ann Ogle Tayloe had 15 children, 13 who lived to adulthood, so why so many tales of tragic deaths giving rise to ghosts should have attached themselves to this one site and one family remains a mystery. Certainly, the 12 men who determined to stay overnight in 1888 to disprove the existence of Octagon ghosts reconsidered their scepticism when, to their horror, the house was suddenly filled with three female shrieks. Could it be the agonized ghost of a slave woman who once worked in the house and who may have been secretly murdered? Why would the bells hanging in the kitchen ring of their own accord? Why, when a visiting gentleman attempted to silence them,

was he lifted bodily from the floor? And what of the magnificent spiral staircase that winds its way from the main floor all the way to the top? A doctor making a house call here in the 1950s encountered a man on the stairway dressed in an early 19th-century military uniform. The mysterious soldier may be looking for one of the Tayloe daughters, who supposedly loved a soldier named Richard Manners. Racing to a rendezvous with him in the garden one night, the girl tripped and plunged over the stairway railing to her death. Her ghost is said to appear on the stairway on 'the night when the silver light of a full moon filters in through the windows'. Other accounts describe a quarrel between Colonel John Tayloe and one of his daughters that took place on the stairway. Again, the body of a young women careens over the stair rail and is discovered listless on the floor below. Was it an accident? Was it suicide? Was she pushed? It was certainly sinister, because when this ghost manifests itself the sounds of whispers in angry tones are heard, followed by the sound of falling.

THE OCTAGON;
GROUP TOURS AVAILABLE (ARRANGEMENTS TO BE MADE IN ADVANCE);
www.archfoundation.org/octagon

7 To return to Farragut West Metro station, exit the garden and return to 18th Street, NW. Turn right and follow 18th Street five blocks to the corner of 18th and I Streets, NW. The 18th Street entrance to the station will be on your left.

An Oasis of Peace and Calm

Nestled atop a leafy rise in northwest Washington are enormous Victorian homes bejewelled in architectural splendour.

When you feel the need to escape the pavement and office buildings of busy downtown Washington, there is no better course of action than to take the Metro to Cleveland Park. Walking the shady, curving streets in this part of town makes you feel like you're strolling through a New England summer resort. Decorative details proliferate on the late 19th-century houses, with their timber frames and cladding and sporting turrets, towers, oriel and bay windows, steep gables and tall chimneys. It's not hard to imagine yourself sitting on one of the verandas sipping lemonade. An art deco moment – with a look at one of the last period cinemas in Washington – precedes your entry into the world of Queen Anne-style magnificence, when you climb up the Newark Street hill to see home after home built as summer residences for wealthy Washingtonians between 1860 and 1910. Finally, you'll visit one of the most stunning sites in the city: Mount St Alban and the Washington National Cathedral.

As you leave the Cleveland Park Metro station's west exit, notice Sam's Park and Shop, an early car-oriented shopping centre, across the street. Turn right and walk to the Uptown Theater. It will be on your right at 3426 Connecticut Avenue, NW.

Opened by Warner Bros. in October 1936, the historic Uptown Theater – an old-style 'movie palace' – was the creation of architect John Zink, who designed numerous art deco and art moderne cinemas across the US between 1930 and 1945. The Uptown boasts the largest film screen in the city. In 1968, Stanley Kubrick's *2001: A Space Odyssey* premiered here and enjoyed a 51-week run. In 1997, the Uptown hosted the re-release of the *Star Wars* saga. So intent were Washington residents to experience the trilogy at the Uptown, on opening day the queue of ticket-buyers wrapped around the block, turned the corner, and continued several blocks away.

2 Continue along Connecticut Avenue past the Uptown Theater. You will pass the Cleveland Park branch of the District of Columbia (DC) Public Library. When trams began to run along Connecticut Avenue in the late 19th century, the Cleveland Park Company – a residential developer – built a waiting area where the library now stands. Turn right onto Newark Street, NW walking uphill and then on towards No. 3035.

Newark Street was the first road to be developed in what became a new Washington suburb. It looks very much the same today as it did when this Queen Anne-style house was constructed in 1898. Robert Thompson Head was the architect and is responsible for at least 17 houses in the area. Most of the family houses were built between 1894 and 1930.

3 Follow Newark Street to Highland Place, NW. Turn right and stop in front of 3141 and then 3155 Highland Place, both located on the right side of the street.

Both of these residences were designed by architect Robert I. Fleming in 1895 and were the first to appear on Highland Place. In 1894, landscape architect Frederick Law Olmsted advised the federal government on how best to extend Washington's streets beyond the city's original boundaries. Olmsted recommended that the streets that run through Cleveland Park between Connecticut Avenue and 34th Street, NW conform to the natural terrain. This is why streets like Highland Place meander rather than adhere to the strict grid pattern found throughout much of Washington. No. 3209 Highland Place, built in 1906 in the Georgian Revival style, was the first brick house to be constructed in Cleveland Park.

4 From Highland Place turn left onto 33rd Place, NW. On the corner of 33rd Place and Newark Street is 3301 Newark Street.

DISTANCE 1 mile (1.6km)

ALLOW 2 hours

START Cleveland Park Metro station (west exit)

FINISH Olmsted Woods

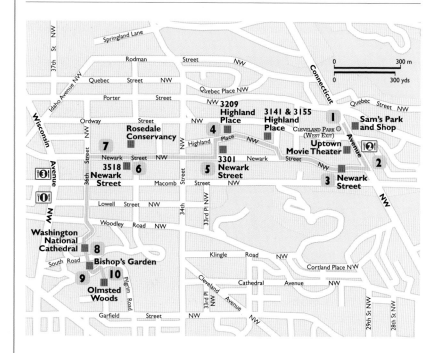

Paul Pelz, designer of the Library of Congress, was one of two architects for this Italian-villa-style residence built by the Cleveland Park Company. John Sherman was the company's president and made a point of hiring Pelz and other well-known architects to create an enclave of unique and impressive properties. Sherman and his artist wife, Ella Bennett Sherman, designed some of the residences themselves. The area you will walk through next was subdivided into a grid pattern in 1894. The curving streets and irregularly shaped plots of land on which the houses in Highland Place were built give way to a more uniform look. The Cleveland Park Company developed many homes in this part of town.

5 Continue on Newark Street to the intersection of 34th Street, NW. Cross 34th Street with caution (there are no traffic lights). Stay on Newark Street until you reach a small gate at No. 3501 on the right. You'll see a stairway of stones ascending the hill to the Rosedale estate.

The oldest house in Cleveland Park is Rosedale, located on the rise above the meadow. The original stone structure dates from about 1740, but in 1794 General Uriah Forrest and his wife, Rebecca, bought the property and added a timber-framed extension. Forrest had fought in the War of American Independence (1775–83), was later Mayor of Georgetown and then a member of Congress. His descendants lived in the house until 1917. By 1959, Rosedale had become a dormitory for girls attending the National Cathedral School. Later, it was used by the non-profit organization Youth for Understanding, which used the house from the late 1970s until 2000. The Friends of Rosedale was founded to ensure the property did not fall into the hands of developers eager to obliterate its historic character and open spaces. In 2004, following an intense fundraising effort and much legal wrangling, the citizens of Cleveland Park purchased the property, creating a land trust known as the Rosedale Conservancy. The Forrest farmhouse has been restored to virtually the same floor plan as existed in the early 1800s, after the Forrests' extension work was carried out.

ROSEDALE CONSERVANCY;

MON–FRI, 7–SUNSET;

www.rosedaleconservancy.org

6 Across the street from Rosedale on Newark Street is No. 3518.

The stone wall that runs just beyond this property is all that remains of Red Top (also known as Oak View), President Grover Cleveland's summer home. Cleveland was one of many wealthy Washingtonians who traded the heat of the city for the shade and serenity of the highland area north of the city centre. Cleveland's tenure here gave this district its name. He bought a stone farmhouse and updated it by adding wooden Victorian porches, a shingled roof and a distinct double chimney. The house was razed to the ground in 1927 and the stones from the house were used to build this wall.

WHERE TO EAT

CAFÉ DELUXE,
3228 Wisconsin Avenue, NW;
Tel: 1-202-686-2233.
American bistro that serves familiar dishes such as meatloaf, chicken pot pie, and pasta with a twist. **$$**

DINO,
3435 Connecticut Avenue, NW;
Tel: 1-202-686-2966.
Dino Gold and his wife, Kay, preside over this homey Italian cafe featuring pasta, light dishes and an inventive wine list. **$$**

TWO AMYS,
2715 Macomb Street, NW;
Tel: 1-202-885-5700.
A wood-burning oven yields authentic Neapolitan pizza at this wildly popular Cleveland Park favourite. **$$**

7 Proceed along Newark Street to the intersection of 36th Street. Turn left on 36th Street and continue through the intersections of Macomb and Lowell Streets, NW and then Woodley Road, NW. Cross Woodley Road and climb the short hill onto the grounds of the Washington National Cathedral.

On 6 January 1893, Congress granted a charter to the Protestant Episcopal Cathedral Foundation of the District of Columbia, allowing it to establish a cathedral and institutions of higher learning. In September 1907, the foundation stone was laid on land called Mount St Alban, the most commanding spot in the city. President Theodore Roosevelt and the Bishop of London addressed the crowd of 10,000. By 1912, the Bethlehem Chapel had opened, but it was not until 1976 that the nave and west rose window were completed; Queen Elizabeth II was present for the dedication. The west towers were completed in September 1990, concluding 83 years of construction. Today, the cathedral and its campus are a hive of activity that includes daily worship services, concerts, exhibitions, talks and guided tours. The legacy of the stone carvers whose work adorns the exterior of the structure in the form of gargoyles and grotesques is the topic of an especially popular tour. Look out for Darth Vader!

WASHINGTON NATIONAL CATHEDRAL;

MON–FRI 10–5.30, SAT 10–4.30, SUN 8–6.30; www.cathedral.org/cathedral

8 On the south side of the cathedral is the enchanting Bishop's Garden.

This terraced landscape features an impressive array of box as well as a recreation of a monastery herb garden from the Middle Ages. Tours of the garden take place on Wednesdays 1 April through to 31 October at 10.30am, except in August. You can pick up a self-guide booklet at the Herb Cottage.

9 Beyond the Bishop's Garden at the base of the Cathedral is the 5-acre (2-hectare) Olmsted Woods.

This is one of the few old forests left in the city. The area has been kept free from development since landscape architect Frederick Law Olmsted Jr designed the cathedral gardens and grounds. The All Hallows Guild, a volunteer group, acts as caretakers of the woodland. Since 1997, the group has been restoring the refuge bit by bit, adding an ecologically sensitive walkway, improving water run-off techniques and adding new plantings.

10 To get to the nearest Metro station, you'll need to take a bus. From the National Cathedral grounds, walk to the intersection of Wisconsin and Cathedral Avenues, NW, where you will see a waiting area for the Metrobus. Any Metrobus numbered 32, 34 or 36 headed in the direction of Friendship Heights will take you to the Tenleytown Metro station, where you can board the red line trains heading into the city centre or Maryland suburbs.

OPPOSITE: STATUE OF GEORGE WASHINGTON INSIDE WASHINGTON NATIONAL CATHEDRAL

Blazing the Sculpture Trail

Three-dimensional artistic expression, from the amusing to the sublime, can be discovered amongst courthouses, fountains and inside a garden.

Outdoor artwork can be found throughout America's capital city, yet perhaps nowhere in such abundance as the area known as Judiciary Square. Why should a place known for its courthouses be the source of so much public artwork? Only the lawyers and judges know for sure, but suffice to say that you will run into some giants of jurisprudence along this route – after you've encountered a 'temple' to an egotistical dentist and two anonymous chess players. The National Gallery of Art East Building – which is itself an outdoor sculpture – provides inspiration for a series of contemporary pieces gracing the museum grounds. Even a federal government agency gets in on the act with a pair of sculptures that embody the art deco movement of the 1930s. You'll conclude at the National Gallery Sculpture Garden, only a decade old and already a favourite outdoor venue. For a quiet ramble away from the populace, take this walk at the weekend, when the courts are closed. Otherwise, for a glimpse of Washington's judicial or municipal hustle and bustle, plan to get there on a weekday.

Exit Archives-Navy Memorial-Penn Quarter Metro station and walk straight across the US Navy Memorial. Notice that you are walking across a map of the world, symbolizing the breadth of a navy's influence.

This memorial was unveiled in October 1987, on the 212th birthday of the US Navy. The most recognized element is probably this statue, *The Lone Sailor*, a composite of the famous Navy bluejacket. The founders of the memorial envisioned the sailor to be around 25 years old, a senior second-class petty officer. His bronze form was created by Stanley Bleifeld, himself a Navy veteran. Artefacts from eight US Navy ships were mixed with the bronze used for the statue. In both form and meaning, then, *The Lone Sailor* embodies the history of the US Navy and its sailors. Before moving on, look at the 26 bronze reliefs framing the memorial that illustrate naval service.

2 Walk down the steps of the memorial, turn left and walk along Pennsylvania Avenue, NW. Cross 7th Street, NW and walk onto the plaza on the other side. Bear left towards the little temple-like edifice.

In 1849, a Connecticut-born dentist named Henry Cogswell headed west to California, hoping to take advantage of the Gold Rush. He invested in property and mining stocks and shares and struck it rich. A loyal adherent to the Temperance Movement, Dr Cogswell decided to donate a fountain to any municipality that would accept one to ensure that passers-by would be able to quench their thirst with water rather than the demon booze. He had the fountains built in his hometown of Bridgeport, Connecticut, underwriting the $4,000 cost to manufacture each one. The fountains varied in size and design, though all featured sculptured marine and animal life; some even featured a bronze portrait of Dr Cogswell himself. Washington's fountain, built in about 1880, was spared that ornamentation in favour of two entwined dolphins and a water crane. Ironically, during the Prohibition in the 1930s the fountain was the domain of a bootlegger known as 'Skats', who reportedly used the fountain as a distribution point for his homemade gin. Later, in the 1960s and 1970s the area immediately adjacent was home to a highly successful purveyor of booze.

155

DISTANCE 1 mile (1.6km)

ALLOW 1.5 hours

START Archives-Navy Memorial-Penn Quarter Metro station

FINISH Archives-Navy Memorial-Penn Quarter Metro station

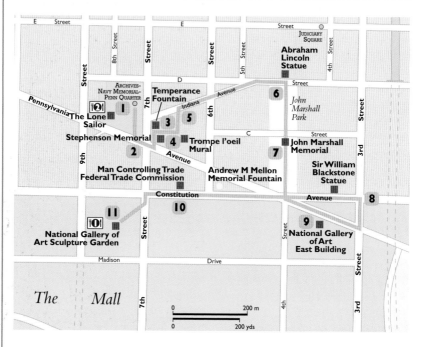

3 Closer to Pennsylvania Avenue on this same plaza you will see a tall, three-sided granite shaft.

A veterans' organization, the Grand Army of the Republic, erected a shrine to its founder, Dr Benjamin F. Stephenson, a surgeon in the US Civil War (1861–65). Sculptor John Massey Rhine created the piece in 1909. The Grand Army was a national society composed of honourably discharged Union soldiers and sailors and was dedicated to assisting permanently

disabled soldiers as well as Union widows. It passed out of existence in 1959 when Albert Woolson, the last remaining Union veteran, died at the age of 109.

4 Just beyond the Stephenson Grand Army of the Republic memorial you can see a light-coloured stone building, which is a bank. Walk to the back of it.

The National Bank of Washington building was constructed in 1889 and designed by Washington architect James

G. Hill. A portion of the building is used by the Argentine Naval Attache. The back of the bank building delights those who notice the trompe l'oeil mural.

5 Bear right towards Indiana Avenue, NW. Follow it to 6th Street, NW, crossing that street and continuing on Indiana Avenue past the Moultrie Courthouse. After you cross the intersection of 5th Street, NW proceed half a block.

This marble statue of America's 16th president, Abraham Lincoln (1809–65), was unveiled in April 1868, three years after his assassination by John Wilkes Booth. Almost immediately after Lincoln's death was announced, a fundraising campaign began to erect a statue in front of the City Hall in Washington. Sculptor Lot Flannery received the commission for what became the first public monument to Lincoln. Unlike the more famous depiction of the president at the Lincoln Memorial, where his monumental size and solid stance evoke his legacy as the leader who held the country together during its darkest years, here the viewer encounters the man who served first as lawyer and then as statesman.

6 Cross Indiana Avenue and make your way through the open terraced space known as John Marshall Park. After you descend the steps to the park proper, notice the small bubbling fountain on the right paying tribute to a natural spring that once flowed in Judiciary Square.

It is not surprising that the memorial dominating John Marshall Park should be none other than the site's namesake. Marshall (1755–1835) was one of the most renowned, influential chief justices of the Supreme Court as well as the founder of judicial review. He served on the court for 34 years, strengthening American Constitution law through myriad far-reaching decisions. Marshall remains a giant – if not the giant – of American jurisprudence. To the left of the John Marshall statue are two

157

WHERE TO EAT

🍽 PAVILION CAFÉ,
National Gallery of Art
(Sculpture Garden),
7th Street and Constitution
Avenue, NW;
Tel: 1-202-289-3361 (extension 5).
Enjoy gourmet salads and sandwiches
on the patio overlooking the
sculptures and fountain. $$

🍽 D'AQUA,
801 Pennsylvania Avenue, NW;
Tel: 1-202-783-7717.
Freshly prepared seafood is the star
of this light-filled Italian restaurant.
The outdoor seating overlooks the
US Navy memorial and the majestic
National Archives. $$$

gentlemen seated on a short retaining wall. They have been engaged in the eleventh move of their chess match since this sculpture was placed here in 1983. The position on the board is taken from an actual game played in 1855 by chess sensation Paul Morphy and his boyhood friend Charles Maurian. Sculptor Lloyd Lillie, however, depicts a scenario in which, at least this time, the chess master would not be savouring victory.

7 Continue through Marshall Park to Pennsylvania Avenue, NW. Turn left and proceed to the plaza in front of the E. Barrett Prettyman Federal Courthouse.

The ceremonial wig worn by this stern-looking figure provides a hint that the lawyer depicted was British. His name was Sir William Blackstone, and he holds a copy of his milestone work, *Commentaries on the Laws of England* (published 1765–69), which clarified English law and aided the individuals who drafted the United States Constitution. This statue was given to the US by the wife of sculptor Paul Wayland Bartlett to celebrate the ties that bind the US and Britain. Mrs Bartlett's original intent was to make the statue a gift from the American Bar Association to the English Bar Association. However, it was discovered that the sculpture, at 9ft (2.7m) high, was too large to stand alongside the other statues in the Hall of Courts in London. Mr Wayland was accommodating and designed a smaller replica for England.

8 Cross Pennsylvania Avenue at 3rd Street, NW. Turn right and walk along the north façade of the National Gallery of Art East Building.

Completed in 1976 and designed by world-famous architect I. M. Pei, the National Gallery of Art East Building has sprinkled its exterior grounds with a variety of contemporary sculpture, the most arresting being *Prinz Friedrich von Homburg, Ein Schauspiel, 3X* by American artist Frank Stella and created 1998–2001. It is a whirlwind of curving aluminium and fibreglass. The title of the work refers to the 19th-century play *Prinz Friedrich von Homburg*, written by the German writer Heinrich von Kleist. Outside the entrance to the East Building stands *Knife Edge Mirror Two Piece* by British artist Henry Moore (1898–1986). Each summer, the National Gallery staff give the piece a good scrubbing to minimize the detrimental effects of its outdoor location. It's an elaborate undertaking: at least six people work for a minimum of three days using mechanical lifts, scaffolding and ladders.

9 Return to Pennsylvania Avenue, turn left, and proceed to the intersection of that street and Constitution Avenue, NW. Proceed and cross 6th Street, NW, continuing along Constitution Avenue to the Federal Trade Commission Building.

This structure is sometimes called the Apex Building for its position in a large precinct known as the Federal Triangle. It is endearing, however, that the true apex is not the building but the daycare playground in its grounds. Two limestone statues, each 12ft (3.6m) high, flank the façade. *Man Controlling Trade* reflects the art deco style of the 1930s and depicts a man controlling a horse, symbolic of the Federal Trade Commission controlling monopolies. Michael Lantz, a young Works Progress Administration instructor from New Rochelle, New York, won the competition to design two sculptures for the Apex in 1942. The Works Progress Administration (WPA) was the largest of the New Deal reforms created by President Franklin D. Roosevelt (1882–1945) in the 1930s.

10 Follow Constitution Avenue across 7th Street. Cross 7th Street and enter the National Gallery of Art Sculpture Garden using the entrance found at 7th Street and Constitution Avenue.

Washington's most recent full-scale viewing ground for outdoor sculpture opened in 1999. Depending on what time of year you visit, you will see either ice-skaters gliding across a frozen rink or arching jets of water spewing forth from a fountain. Abstract and representational work can be found here by such artists as Claes Oldenburg (born 1929), Magdalena Abakanowicz (born 1930), Barry Flanagan (born 1941) and Roy Lichtenstein (born 1923), whose painted aluminium *House I* is a favourite. It is not unusual to be standing near another popular piece, *Typewriter Erase, Scale X*, and hear people from an older generation attempting to explain to their youthful companions how exactly this object was once used. An entrance from a Paris Métro station adds a whimsical element to the patio adjacent to the cafe. Free jazz concerts take place on Friday evenings from May to September.

11 To return to Archives-Navy Memorial-Penn Quarter Metro, exit the National Gallery Sculpture Garden via the entrance near the corner of 7th Street and Constitution Avenue, NW. Cross Constitution Avenue via 7th Street and continue one block to Pennsylvania Avenue, NW. Cross Pennsylvania Avenue and walk half a block along 7th Street.

Washington's Niche Museums

This walk is perfect to take on a cold, rainy day or when the oppressive humidity of Washington's summer makes touring outdoors less desirable.

One could easily spend days roaming through the galleries of the Smithsonian museums lining the National Mall. Yet worthy of your time though they are, a surprising array of smaller institutions can be discovered scattered throughout the city. The four museums included in this walk all focus on a particular subject and are situated in Washington's Penn Quarter, which translates into abundant opportunities for food, drink and entertainment after a morning or afternoon of exhibit viewing. Begin in the heart of Penn Quarter with what must be Washington's smallest museum and one dedicated to that smallest of objects, the bead. Trade the world of handicrafts for a microscope and genomes at one of the city's newest museums, dedicated to explaining breakthroughs in scientific research to the layman. Then honour the life and death of the everyday American hero, the police officer, at a visitor centre and memorial located amidst Washington's federal and city courts. Finally, celebrate architecture and the art of building construction when you enter one of the most spectacular spaces in the city.

Exit Archives-Navy Memorial-Penn Quarter Metro station and head along the path that wraps around the US Navy memorial. Turn right onto D Street, NW, then stop at the intersection of 7th and D Streets, NW.

In 1983, 12 bead enthusiasts founded the Bead Society of Greater Washington. By 1995, the organization had created a museum, with individuals contributing to the collection, and set up various national bead societies. A centrepiece of the viewing experience is the Bead Timeline of History, which employs beads and beaded ornaments to 'bridge geographic, socio-economic, and cultural divides suggesting common ground among diverse communities'. An advantage of the Bead Museum's small size is that a knowledgeable staff person is always close at hand, willing to offer explanations or answer questions – and probably working on a beading project to boot!

THE BEAD MUSEUM;

TUE–SAT 12–6;

www.beadmuseumdc.org

2 Next door at 700 7th Street is the National Law Enforcement Officers memorial visitors centre.

This gift shop and information centre complements the National Law Enforcement Officers memorial located a few blocks away. You will see photographs of the memorial itself, including a wall-length mural of the opening ceremonies in 1991 and a rare photo of the memorial site and its surroundings as they appeared in 1890. Touching mementos left at the memorial by friends and loved ones are on display. An interactive video system allows visitors to read brief biographies and view a photograph of the individual police officers honoured, along with their respective location on the memorial walls. Exhibits such as one about the life and times of Wyatt Earp (1848–1929) – the American folk hero and officer of the law in various Western frontier towns, best known for his involvement in the Gunfight at the OK Corral – provide a historic context to American law enforcement; 'The Deadliest Day in Law Enforcement History – September 11, 2001' presents its dangers in stark relief.

NATIONAL LAW ENFORCEMENT OFFICERS MEMORIAL (VISITORS CENTRE);

MON–FRI 9–5, SAT 10–5, SUN 12–5;

TEL: 1-202-737-3213;

www.nleomf.com/TheMemorial/visitorscenter.htm

OPPOSITE: THE NATIONAL LAW ENFORCEMENT OFFICERS MEMORIAL; ABOVE: THE BEAD MUSEUM

DISTANCE I mile (1.6km)

ALLOW I hour for walk (plus at least 2 hours to include museum visits)

START Archives-Navy Memorial-Penn Quarter Metro station

FINISH Judiciary Square Metro station

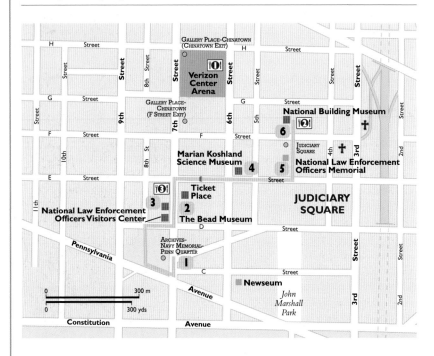

3 Cross 7th Street at D Street. Turn left and walk one block to E Street, NW. Take note of Ticket Place, where you can purchase discounted tickets to many Washington theatre performances. On reaching E Street, NW, follow it to the end of the block. Cross 6th Street, NW. At the corner of 6th and E Streets is the entrance to the Marian Koshland Science Museum.

Since it opened in 2004, this museum has sought to engage the general public in 'science behind the headlines'. The Koshland was set up in memory of one woman's passion for science – immunologist and molecular biologist Marian 'Bunny' Koshland (1921–97). She once wrote in the *Annual Reviews of Immunology* that she chose science as a career because it was a means of making lasting, if not immortal, contributions to humankind. True to her calling, she went on to conduct groundbreaking research in the behaviour of antibodies. Her husband, Daniel

Koshland (1920–2007), also a renowned molecular biologist, partnered with the National Academy of Sciences to found this museum through a monetary gift he made to continue his wife's legacy.

MARIAN KOSHLAND SCIENCE MUSEUM;

DAILY (EXCEPT TUE) 10–6;

TEL: 1-202-334-1201;

www.koshland-science-museum.org

4 From the museum, turn left and walk along E Street, crossing 5th Street, NW. Look across 5th Street to see the large globe balanced atop the National Academies Building. Continue on E Street for half a block. You've now entered an area of the city known as Judiciary Square.

In this quiet district of Washington, the US honours its police officers – the men and women who day in and day out patrol the streets, who have regular contact with citizenry of all sorts, and who valiantly enforce the laws that shore up big cities and small towns alike. The memorial was unveiled in 1991 and occupies 3 acres (1.2 hectares) of Judiciary Square, the place that has been the site of the federal and city judicial buildings almost since Washington's founding. At the entrance are statuary groupings of an adult lion protecting its cubs. Sculpted by Raymond Kaskey (born 1943), they symbolize the protective role played by law officers in today's society. Inscribed on marble walls along the paths are the randomly placed names of more than 17,500 officers

WHERE TO EAT

🍽 BURMA,
740 6th Street, NW;
Tel: 1-202-638-1280.
Located upstairs, this no-frills Burmese restaurant offers especially tasty appetizers and Asian salads. $

🍽 HIGH NOON,
National Building Museum,
401 F Street NW;
Tel: 1-202-628-0906.
Even a humble sandwich is raised to new heights when eaten in the spectacular space that is the National Building Museum's Great Hall. $

🍽 JALEO,
480 7th Street, NW;
Tel: 1-202-628-7949.
José Andrés is one of Washington's first celebrity chefs. He made his name initially by creating the tapas served at this restaurant. $$

who have been killed in the line of duty, dating back to the first known death in 1792. At an annual candlelight vigil held each year during National Police Week (in May), new names of fallen officers are added.

NATIONAL LAW ENFORCEMENT OFFICERS MEMORIAL;

www.nleomf.com

5 Walk across the National Law Enforcement Officers memorial from E to F Streets. Notice the entrance

to the Judiciary Square Metro station. Cross F Street.

One step inside will quickly reveal why this building always plays host to a presidential inaugural ball. It is one of the most stunning, soaring spaces in Washington. Prior to becoming the National Building Museum in 1980, the building was used as government offices. The 1,200ft- (365m-) long exterior frieze that wraps around the entire building depicts a parade of US Civil War military units, hinting at the original function of the building. Designed in 1881 by civil engineer and US Army General Montgomery C. Meigs, it housed the Pension Bureau. From the beginning, it was praised as a marvel of engineering. A guided tour of the building (highly recommended) will reveal features such as the ingenious system of windows, vents and open archways that allow the structure's Great Hall to function as a reservoir of light and air. Today, visitors to the National Building Museum can explore exhibits dedicated to architecture, design, engineering, construction and urban planning. The museum shop is one of the best in the city.

NATIONAL BUILDING MUSEUM;
MON–SAT 10–5, SUN 11–5;
TEL: 1-202-272-2448; www.nbm.org

6 To end the walk, exit the National Building Museum at F Street, NW. You will find the entrance to the Judiciary Square Metro station just across the street.

ABOVE: THE STUNNING INTERIOR OF THE NATIONAL BUILDING MUSEUM

International Washington

West of the White House are the institutions that bring the international community flooding into America's capital city.

Here is an insider's walk of Washington. Few visitors, or locals for that matter, take the time to notice the hundreds of employees who pour out of the Farragut West Metro station each day on their way to work at the World Bank and International Monetary Fund. What these seven blocks lack in architectural charm or historic structures, they more than make up for in accessibility. Unlike the diplomatic community along Embassy Row, where the policy is look but don't drop in, the international agencies featured on this walk provide venues expressly for the public to visit, so take this walk during the working week when the offices are open. This route, though, isn't all about work and office buildings: you'll wander through a park or two – even a tiny sculpture garden – and you'll see a beautiful row of stately Beaux Arts headquarters. A stroll through the George Washington University campus, with its large population of international students, concludes this outing through an area of Washington where all the world's nations seem to be represented in the passers-by.

| Exit Farragut West Metro station onto 18th Street, NW and turn right, crossing I Street, NW. Halfway down the block on the left is Taberna del Alabardero.

One of the most beautiful dining rooms in Washington, Taberna del Alabardero ('Tavern of the Palace Guards') began its life in Spain over 25 years ago, when Father Luis de Lezama rented a 16th-century townhouse near the Royal Palace in Madrid. Despite having no prior training in the restaurant business, he began serving meals to great acclaim. In 1989, Lezama crossed the Atlantic to open Taberna del Alabardero in Washington. Other outposts of the restaurant can be found in Seville and Benahavis in Spain. Those craving an escape to Old World Spain via the US capital city need only head through the doors of Taberna del Alabardero for sherry, tapas and incomparable paella.

Street, helps to heighten public awareness of the organization's role in the global economy via permanent and changing exhibits, a bookstore and gift shop.

IMF CENTER;
MON–FRI 10–4.30;
www.imf.org/external/np/exr/center

2 Continue on 18th Street to the intersection of H Street, NW. Turn right and then turn left onto 19th Street, NW. After crossing Pennsylvania Avenue, NW you will cross H Street again. Continue on 19th Street until you reach the International Monetary Fund at No. 700.

An international organization of 185 member countries, the International Monetary Fund (IMF) was founded to promote monetary cooperation as well as to provide temporary financial assistance to countries. Its IMF Center, at 720 19th

3 Return to H Street and turn right. The World Bank is located at 1818 H Street.

Conceived during World War II at Bretton Woods, New Hampshire, the World Bank initially helped rebuild Europe after the war. Its first loan of $250 million was to France in 1947 for post-war reconstruction. Such activity has remained a focus of the bank's work, though its mission has evolved to include the alleviation of global poverty. Being an international enterprise, 40 per cent of the staff work abroad.

167

DISTANCE 1.5 miles (2.5km)

ALLOW 1.5 hours (more with site visits)

START Farragut West Metro station (18th Street, NW exit)

FINISH Foggy Bottom Metro station

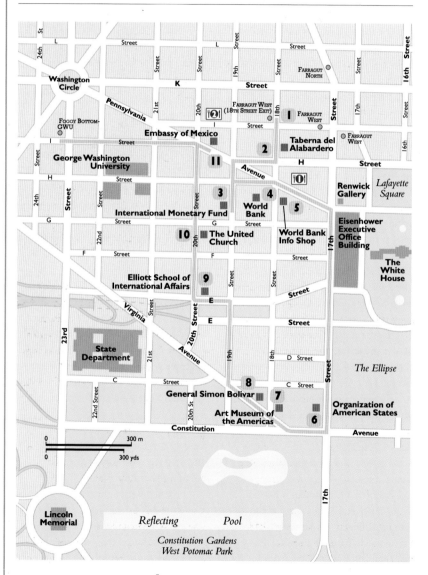

4 Follow H Street to the intersection of 18th Street. Across the street on the corner is the World Bank Info Shop.

The public can delve into the mission of the World Bank by visiting InfoShop. World Bank publications are available for perusal or purchase and computer work stations allow users to browse World Bank websites and databases. Shop staff will even provide a guided tour of its resources.

WORLD BANK INFOSHOP;
MON–FRI 9–5; www.worldbank.org/infoshop

5 Turn right onto Pennsylvania Avenue from InfoShop and then right again onto 17th Street, NW. For the next five blocks, you'll pass majestic edifices constructed in the Beaux Arts style at the turn of the 20th century: the grandiose Eisenhower Executive Office Building is first, followed by the Corcoran Gallery of Art, the Red Cross headquarters and the Daughters of the American Revolution. At the intersection of 17th Street and Constitution Avenue, NW is the stately Organization of American States.

A 1966 sculpture of Queen Isabella I of Spain (1451–1504) greets visitors arriving at the Organization of American States (OAS). She is remembered in the US as the queen who pawned her jewels to finance the first voyage of Christopher Columbus in 1492, popularly described as the 'discoverer' of the New World. The OAS, which was set up in 1948, functions as a forum for strengthening democracy, promoting human rights

WHERE TO EAT

|O| BREADLINE,
1751 Pennsylvania Avenue, NW;
Tel: 1-202-822-8900.
Whatever you select at this busy takeaway, make sure it includes the delicious bread baked on the premises. The sandwiches, salads and soups are all excellent. Closed at weekends. $

|O| KAZ SUSHI BISTRO,
1915 I Street, NW;
Tel: 1-202-530-5500.
One of the top spots for sushi in the city. Japanese businessmen vie for one of the six chairs at the bar to watch chef Kaz and his staff prepare the day's selection. $$

and confronting shared problems such as poverty, terrorism and illegal drugs in the Americas. There are 35 member states from North, Central and South America, as well as Caribbean nations. Proceedings are conducted in the four official languages of the OAS – English, Spanish, Portuguese and French.

6 Turn right onto Constitution Avenue and then right again onto 18th Street. At the corner is the Art Museum of the Americas.

In 1976, the OAS established this museum as a tribute to America's bicentenary. The building was designed by architect Paul Cret in 1912, originally

unveiled in 1959, is one of the largest equestrian statues in the US. It was designed by Austrian-born US sculptor Felix W. de Weldon, who also created the Iwo Jima Memorial near Arlington National Cemetery in Virginia, just across the Potomac River from Washington. Bolivar was one of the most important leaders of Hispanic America's successful struggle for independence from Spain. He participated in the foundation of the Gran Colombia, a nation forming the liberated Spanish colonies, becoming its president from 1821 to 1830. The Gran Colombia dissolved in 1831, yet Bolivar's legacy contributed to the independence of present-day Bolivia, Colombia, Ecuador, Panama, Peru and Venezuela.

8 Facing the statue, turn left on Virginia Avenue and then right onto 19th Street. Proceed to a small park bounded by E Street, NW on both its south and north. Turn left on the northern side and look for 1957 E Street, which will be on the right.

as the residence for the OAS Secretaries General. The museum's permanent collection of 20th-century Latin American and Caribbean art is one of the most significant in the country. Make sure to amble through the small sculpture garden found in the grounds.

ART MUSEUM OF THE AMERICAS;

TUE–SUN 10–5; www.museum.oas.org

7 Across 18th Street from the museum on Virginia Avenue is an equestrian statue of General Simon Bolivar.

At 27ft (8m) high, this bronze figure of General Simon Bolivar (1783–1830),

One of the primary reasons that undergraduate and graduate students select Washington for their education is the opportunity to earn a degree from George Washington University's Elliott School of International Affairs. In 1898, what was then Columbian College opened its School of Jurisprudence and Diplomacy, the precursor to the Elliott School. At the time, the study of international affairs was considered useful for

ABOVE: BRONZE EQUESTRIAN STATUE OF SIMON BOLIVAR

training future diplomats or international lawyers. By the 1920s, emphasis on international business was added. Today, the university prepares its students not only for careers in public service, perhaps with the US State Department, but also in the private sector and non-governmental organizations such as the World Bank and International Monetary Fund (IMF). Degree courses include the Master of International Policy and Practice and Master of International Trade and Investment Policy. Regional study programmes cover Europe, Russia, Southeast Asia, Latin America, Canada and the Caribbean. The Elliot School has professional and education partnerships with over a dozen universities around the world.

9 Continue on E Street to 20th Street, NW. Turn right and proceed one block. At the corner of 20th and G Streets is the United Church.

In 1833, the Evangelical Concordia Congregation built a red-brick Romanesque Revival church on this site to accommodate the German immigrants who had begun to arrive in Washington; many took up residence in this area known as Foggy Bottom. A few years later, a small group of Methodists established the Union Methodist Episcopal Church nearby. By January 1975, the two congregations had decided to merge, forming the United Church, or *Vereinigte Kirche*. A German-language worship service is held twice a month.

10 Proceed on 20th Street until it intersects with Pennsylvania Avenue. Turn right and look for No. 1911 across the street, the Embassy of Mexico.

The two countries that border the US each have an embassy on Pennsylvania Avenue, with Canada's located between the White House and US Capitol. In addition, both nations have numerous consulates and other facilities across the US. A portion of the Mexican Embassy is housed in what remains of the Seven Buildings, a row of houses once considered the most prestigious residential address in Washington. After they were developed in 1796, the residences were home to government officials and foreign ministers, who valued the property's close proximity to the White House and Georgetown. The State Department operated from one of the buildings when the federal government arrived in 1800; President and Mrs James Madison lived in a unit while the White House was being rebuilt following its burning by the British during the War of 1812. By the 1890s, many of the houses had begun to be used commercially. In 1959, some of the units were razed for an office building, and, in a rather unfortunate finale, the two surviving houses were enveloped by the massive office complex now in use as the Mexican Embassy.

11 To end the walk, double back to 20th Street and turn left onto I Street. Foggy Bottom station is three blocks away.

THE ATRIUM OF THE WORLD BANK HEADQUARTERS

INDEX

Adams, Abigail 146
Adams, Henry 50, 54
African-American Civil War
    Memorial 110
American Civil War 61, 66–71,
    72, 73, 110
Art Museum of the Americas
    169–70
Arthur Sackler Gallery 130,
    131
Artifactory Building 79

Barney House 124, 127
Barry, John 93
Barton, Clara 69
Bead Museum 161
Ben's Chili Bowl 107, 110
Berliner, Emile 80
Bethune, Mary McLeod 18,
    95–6
Birch Funeral Home and
    Stable 10
Bishop's Garden 153
Blackstone, Sir William 158
Blair House 55
Bohemian Caverns 109–10
Bolivar, Simon 170
Bomford Mill 13
Booth, John Wilkes 51, 70,
    76–7, 145
Bradlee, Ben 138, 140
Brady, Mathew 67–8, 69
Brewmaster's Castle 113
Bureau of Engraving and
    Printing 23–4

Cairo Hotel 116
Canadian Embassy 42–3
Capitol Hill 14–19, 58–65
Capitol Hill Club 59
Cecil Place 12–13
cherry trees 22, 27, 28
Chesapeake & Ohio Canal

9–11, 12
Chinatown 43, 81
Church of Scientology 117
Cleveland, Grover 151
Cleveland Park 148–53
Clinton, Bill 57
Cluss, Adolf 47, 93
Cogswell, Henry 155
Columbia Residences 87
Constitution Avenue 35
Cosmos Club 124

Dean & DeLuca 13, 137
Decatur Place 101
Devore Chase 105
Dumbarton House 45
Dumbarton Oaks 48–9
Dupont Circle 112–19, 122

East Capitol Street 17–18
Eastern Market 19
Eisenhower Executive Office
    Building 55, 56, 57
Ellington, 'Duke' 106, 107,
    108, 111
Elliott School of International
    Affairs 170–1
Emancipation Monument 18,
    20–1
Embassy Row 120–7
Enid Haupt Garden 130
Environmental Protection
    Agency Building 35
Everett House 124
Evermay 45–6

Federal Bureau of Investigation
    (FBI) 41–2
Federal Trade Commission
    Building 159
Foggy Bottom 84–91
Folger Shakespeare Library 17
Ford's Theatre 70, 71, 76–7

Franklin D. Reeves Center for
    Municipal Affairs 111
Franklin School 93
Fraunz House 18
Freedom Plaza 39–40
Freer Gallery of Art 129,
    134–5
French Ambassador's
    Residence 102

Georgetown 8–13, 44–9,
    136–41
Grace Episcopal Church 12
Graham, Katharine 46–7
Grand Army of the Republic
    Memorial 67, 156
Grant, Ulysses S. 51, 61, 62
Greater New Hope Baptist
    Church 81

Hancock, General Winfield
    Scott 67
Hanna, Mark 51
Harriman, Pamela 140
Hay-Adams Hotel 54
Henry, Joseph 132
Highland Place 149, 150
Hirshhorn Museum 133
Holy Rosary Catholic Church
    83
Holy Trinity Church (St
    Ignatius Chapel) 139
Hoover, J. Edgar 41–2
Hope Diamond 123
Hotel Monaco 79
Hotel Tabard Inn 114–15

Industrial Bank 108–9
International Monetary Fund
    (IMF) 167
International Order of the
    Eastern Star 117

J. Edgar Hoover Building 41–2
Jackson, Andrew 52, 53, 54, 145
Jefferson, Thomas 25, 31, 38, 63, 146
Jefferson Pier Stone 31–2
Jewish Washington 81–2, 83
John F. Kennedy Center for the Performing Arts 88, 89, 90–1
John Marshall Park 157–8
John Wilson Building 39
Johnson, Andrew 51, 57
Judiciary Square 154, 157, 163

Kalorama 100–5
Kennedy, Jacqueline 85, 137, 138, 140, 141
Kennedy, John F. 62, 136, 137, 138, 139–40
King, Martin Luther 28, 34, 39–40, 107, 111
Korean War Veterans Memorial 33, 36–7
Kutz Bridge 28

Lafayette, Marquis de 52
Lafayette Square 50–7, 142–7
Laird-Dunlop House 140
Library of Congress Jefferson Building 63
Library Court 16
Lillian and Albert Small Jewish Museum 83
Lincoln, Abraham 18, 34, 51, 66, 68, 70, 71, 72, 73–4, 75, 76–7, 145, 146, 157
Lincoln Memorial 34
Lincoln Park 18
Lincoln Theater 107
Lindens 103
Logan, John A. 96
Logan Circle 92, 95–7
Lucas, Anthony 101
Luther Place Memorial Church 95

McKinley, William 51
McPherson, Major General James 73
Madison, Dolly 45, 143, 145
The Maples 15
Marian Koshland Science Museum 162–3
markets 13, 19, 112, 113
Mary McLeod Bethune Council House 95
Mary Ripley Garden 132–3
Mason, George 27, 29
Mexican Embassy 43, 171
Montgomery, Helen 137
Montrose Park 48

National Air Force Memorial 27
National Archives 42
National Bank of Washington 156–7
National Building Museum 164–5
National City Christian Church 93, 95
National Council of Negro Women 67–8
National Democratic Club 59
National Gallery of Art 42, 133, 158–9
National Law Enforcement Officers Memorial 161, 163
National Mall 22
National Museum of African Art 130, 131
National Museum of American Jewish Military History 117
National Trust for Historic Preservation 113–14
National World War II Memorial 32–3
Naval Lodge Building 15
New York Avenue Presbyterian Church 76
Newark Street 149, 150–1, 153
Newseum 43

Nixon, Richard 57
North, Oliver 57

Oak Hill Cemetery 47
Octagon 147
Old Post Office 41
Old Stone House 13
Olmsted Woods 153
Organization of American States (OAS) 169
Our Lady, Queen of the Americas Church 101

Patterson House/Washington Club 121
Penn Quarter 78–83, 160
Pennsylvania Avenue 38–43, 85, 87
Petersen House 71, 77
Phillips Collection 126, 127
Powell, Lewis 51, 75
Prayer of Columbus 67
Pre-Columbian Museum 49

Rathbone, Major Henry 74–5, 145–6
Rayburn Building 59
Robert A. Taft Garden Park 61–2
Robert Peter House/Ritz Carlton 11–12
Rodgers House 51
Roosevelt, Alice 122
Roosevelt, Eleanor 127
Roosevelt, Franklin D. 27, 42, 127, 159
Rosedale 151
Russell Caucus Room 62

S. Dillon Ripley Center 129
St John's Church 73–4
St Marks' Episcopal Church 16, 17
St Mary Mother of God Catholic Church 82–3
St Mary's Church 85

St Mary's Court 85
St Patrick's Catholic Church 70
St Thomas Episcopal Church
   115
sculpture trail 154–9
Sewall-Belmont House and
   Museum 62
Seward, William 51, 73, 75, 76
Sickles, Daniel E. 54–5
Signers' Memorial 34
6th and I Synagogue 82
Smithsonian American Art
   Museum 69
Smithsonian Institution/The
   Castle 131
Smithsonian Museum of
   American Art and National
   Portrait Gallery 79–80
Society of the Cincinnati 123,
   125
Stanton, Edwin M. 47, 77
Stephen Decatur House
   Museum 143

Studio Theater 97
Sulgrave Club 113, 121

Taberna del Albardero 167
Tayloe House 51
Thomas Circle 93, 98–9
Thomas Jefferson Memorial 25
Tidal Basin 22, 24–5, 28
True Reformer Building 107–8
Truman, Harry 55
Tudor Place 49

United Church 171
Uptown Theater 149
US Botanic Garden 59–60
US Capitol 58, 60–1, 64–5
US Court of Claims and
   Appeals 51
US Forest Service 23
US Holocaust Memorial
   Museum 23
US Navy Memorial 43, 155
US Supreme Court 62–3

Veteran's Administration
   Building 73
Vietnam Veterans Memorial 34

Wadsworth, Henry and
   Martha 121
Wah Luck House 82
Walsh-McLean House 122
Washington, George 31, 85
Washington Circle 85
Washington Harbor 11
Washington National
   Cathedral 153
Watergate 88
White House 57, 75, 146
Whitelaw apartments 110–11
Whitman, Walt 67, 69
Willard Hotel 39, 76
William Marbury House 137
Wilson, Woodrow 105
Woodrow Wilson House 105
World Bank 167, 169, 172–3
World War Memorial 33

ACKNOWLEDGEMENTS

The Automobile Association wishes to thank the following photographers, companies and picture libraries for their assistance in the preparation of this book.
Abbreviations for the picture credits are as follows – (AA) AA World Travel Library
Front Cover AA/Clive Sawyer; 3 AA/Clive Sawyer; 7 AA/Clive Sawyer; 12 Carolyn Crouch; 14 Alamy/David R. Frazier Photolibrary,Inc.; 17 Topher Mathews; 19 Alamy/Chuck Pefley; 20/21 photolibrary.com/North Wind Picture Archives; 22 dcstockimages.com/Randy Santos; 26 dcstockimages.com/Randy Santos; 29 Alamy/Florida Images; 31 AA/Clive Sawyer; 34 Getty Images/Richard Nowitz; 38 Courtesy of InterContinental Hotels Group; 41 dcstockimages.com/Randy Santos; 43 dcstockimages.com/Randy Santos; 44 Carolyn Crouch; 45 Alamy/Nikreates; 47 Corbis/Kelly-Mooney Photography; 53 Corbis/John Aikins; 56 photolibrary.com/Christy Kanis; 58 dcstockimages.com/Randy Santos; 59 dcstockimages.com/Randy Santos; 63 AA/Clive Sawyer; 64/65 dcstockimages.com/Randy Santos; 66 Alamy/Rich Iwasaki; 69 Carolyn Crouch; 72 Alamy/Rough Guides; 73 Getty Images /AFP; 77 Collinstock/Carol M. Highsmith; 78 dcstockimages.com/Randy Santos; 79 Carolyn Crouch; 84 Alamy/Wim Wiskerke; 88 AA/Clive Sawyer; 90/91 Houserstock/Dave G. Houser; 92 AA/Clive Sawyer; 96 dcstockimages.com/Randy Santos; 98/99 dcstockimages.com/Randy Santos; 100 SuperStock/James Lemass; 103 Carolyn Crouch; 104 Carolyn Crouch; 106 Alamy/Rough Guides; 107 Getty Images /AFP; 109 Alamy/Nikreates; 112 dcstockimages.com/Randy Santos; 116 Susan Isakson/Alamy; 118/119 dcstockimages.com/Randy Santos; 120 Alamy/Carrie Garcia; 125 Carolyn Crouch; 126 Alamy/Michael Ventura ; 128 Getty Images/Jonathan Nourok; 131 AA/Clive Sawyer; 132 Houserstock/Dave G. Houser; 134/135 Alamy/Stock Connection Distribution; 140 Alamy/Chuck Pefley; 141 drr.net/Chuck Pefley; 142 National Geographic/Getty Images; 148 Carolyn Crouch; 154 Carolyn Crouch; 155 Collinstock/Carol M. Highsmith; 157 drr.net/Elliott Teel/Dcstockphoto; 160 Carolyn Crouch; 161 Carolyn Crouch; 167 Collinstock/Carol M. Highsmith; 170 Alamy/Photov.com/Hisham Ibrahim; 172/173 Alamy/Wim Wiskerke.
Every effort has been made to trace copyright holders, and we apologize in advance for any unintentional omissions or errors. We would be pleased to apply any corrections in any following editions of this publication.